I Came From Joy!

Spiritual Affirmations and Activities for Children

Crystal Clarity, Publishers
Nevada City, California

Written and Illustrated by Lorna Ann Knox

I Came From Joy !

Spiritual Affirmations and Activities for Children

ISBN: 1-56589-146-5

Contributing Editor: Susan Dermond
Cover Art: Sarah Brink
Cover Design: Michael Coombs and C. A. Starner Schuppe
Interior Design: Patty Arnold, Andrea Miles,
C. A. Starner Schuppe, and Julia Beinhorn

10 9 8 7 6 5 4 3 2 1
Printed in China

Crystal Clarity, Publishers
14618 Tyler Foote Road
Nevada City, CA 95959-8599

800-424-1055 or 530-478-7600
Fax: 530-478-7610
E-mail: clarity@crystalclarity.com
Website: www.crystalclarity.com

Library of Congress Cataloging-in-Publication Data

Knox, Lorna Ann.
I came from joy : spiritual affirmations and activities for children / written and
illustrated by Lorna Ann Knox.
p.cm.
Include bibliographical references and index.
ISBN 1-56589-146-5 (trade paper)
1. Religious education of children. I. Title.

BL42 .K56 2000
291.7′5′083—dc21
00-031803

Contents

About Lorna Ann Knox

Lorna Ann Knox, BSN is a private school teacher, parent, and director of the Ananda Sunday School in Portland for the last 6 years. She also teaches education workshops for educators and parents. Prior to working with schools, Lorna was a health educator for 15 years and is a certified nurse. She is married and the mother of three children.

Foreword • • • • • • • • • • • • • •

When I began to work with Lorna Knox, a teacher and home-schooling parent, I was immediately struck by her balance of confidence and humility, idealism and practicality, in her manner of dealing with children. Enthusiasm and creative ideas for teaching just bubbled out of Lorna.

Of course, the single most important influence on the character of our children is our example and the magnetism of who we are. But beyond that, how can we share our values with children? How do we motivate children to want to pray, meditate, and listen to their own "inner voices" of conscience and Higher Self?

These questions have occupied me and my colleagues on the Ananda Living Wisdom School (a small, private school in northern California, dedicated to holistic, spiritual education) staff for twelve years. We knew that only a living curriculum—one that provides experiences of inspiration—was really meaningful to children. So we set out to learn to provide those experiences, and to provide them in a way that develops all sides of the child: body, feeling, will power, and intellect. Workshops and books grew out of our discoveries as well as the establishment of other Ananda Living Wisdom Schools.

I was thrilled when I first saw the ideas and illustrations for Lorna's book, *I Came From Joy*, because here was someone who independently had come to all the same conclusions about sharing spirituality with children that we had. Here was an original and beautiful example of a Living Wisdom curriculum that could be used in the classroom, in Sunday school, or even at home with an individual child.

Lorna's delightful assortment of activities, art projects, handouts, and stories make it possible for children of all ages to explore spiritual qualities—love, joy, forgiveness, compassion, courage, patience, will power, kindness (26 qualities in all). Lorna offers her insights without dogmatism, in a spirit of love and respect, encouraging each child to learn at his or her own pace. *I Came From Joy* reflects her understanding, based on years of working with children, that children are naturally attracted to spiritual values when presented in a joyful, nurturing way.

Without hesitation, I would recommend this wonderful book to parents and teachers alike. Use it with love and respect for each child, and you will be delighted by the results!

Blessings to you,

Susan Dermond
Director, Ananda Living Wisdom School
Beaverton, Oregon

Introduction • • • • • • • • • • •

When I took on the role of Sunday school teacher in my small church there was no established curriculum to follow. I found it difficult to put together lesson plans for the small groups of children that constantly varied in number, age, gender and familiarity with our church. For help I turned to *Affirmations for Self-Healing*, by J. Donald Walters. This book gives fifty-two affirmations, each on a different spiritual quality, to use as tools in the work of spiritual growth and healing. Taken together, these 52 qualities define what it means to be a spiritually mature individual.

I used Walters' book as a starting point for a loose-format curriculum that would be adaptable for children spanning a wide age range. First I modified the affirmations so that young children could understand and memorize them easily. Then I developed activities, projects and resources for each spiritual quality. I began to look at scripture readings and children's books differently—in light of the spiritual qualities they highlighted.

When I first used my new format in Sunday school, I worked with only one quality per month. This gave the children and me the chance to explore each quality in depth, and to find out what worked well and what did not. Gradually, the material for this book came together.

I continue to turn to *Affirmations for Self-Healing* when I need help in teaching, or to clarify my personal goals. Donald Walters states in his introduction, "Living, too, is an art." From all indications, Walters practices the art of living with apparent ease. Those who try to do the same soon realize that this apparent ease comes only after years of dedicated effort.

We can make our most valuable contribution to our children's learning and growing by striving to practice the art of living with awareness and love, and by allowing our children to watch and be part of our efforts. Let the children you love see you work at being a better person. Let them see you grow in love and joy as a result, and they will *want* to follow your example.

Lorna Ann Knox
Portland, Oregon
July 2000

Using this book • • • • • • • • • •

This book offers 24 spiritual qualities to be used as lesson topics for teaching spiritual values to children in Sunday schools, public schools, in the home, and also in other settings. Each chapter focuses on a single spiritual quality, and provides classroom activities that use music, art, stories and games to bring the topic into clear focus for the children. There are also reproducible handouts and quotations for teacher study.

Each chapter can be used as a complete lesson plan for a 60 to 90 minute class. You can also create shorter lesson plans by dividing the chapters into segments to be used over a series of days or weeks. A parent teaching at home or looking for fun ways to convey spiritual ideas will also find many helpful and practical ideas here.

Each chapter has six components presented in the following sequence:

INTRODUCING PAGE—This page introduces the spiritual quality. The children's' affirmation and prayer, and a small version of the affirmation picture, also appear on this page. The introducing page can be copied and given to the children to share with parents. When folded it half, it can be placed on a table or mantle.

AFFIRMATION—An affirmation is a statement of truth that can have a great impact on our consciousness if said with concentration and energy. The children's affirmation appears on the introducing page.

PRAYER—Prayer is a way of acknowledging that we need more than self-effort to change. The children's prayer also appears on the introducing page.

EXPLORING—This section follows the introduction page and gives ideas for classroom activities.

UNDERSTANDING—This section, which follows "Exploring," is intended to help the teacher or parent gain a deeper understanding of the spiritual quality.

AFFIRMATION PICTURE—A full page at the end of each chapter is devoted to the affirmation picture.

A further word on these components:

AFFIRMATIONS—

I would urge you to practice each of the children's affirmations before you decide how you will use them with the children. Walters recommends the following approach. First, say the affirmation several times out loud, with energy and conviction. Then repeat the affirmation several times, saying it in ever-quieter tones until you are saying it silently to yourself. Continue to repeat the words silently, at the seat of divine awareness, the point between the eyebrows, known as the Christ center. Spend a few moments in silence or prayer afterwards.

You can follow these same basic steps when you teach the affirmation to children. For younger children, however, you may want to reduce the number of repetitions and also the time spent in silence or prayer. Always make sure that the children really understand all the words of the affirmation. Discussing the topic concept—the spiritual quality being studied—helps to clarify misunderstandings.

The affirmations can be used in a variety of creative ways; you need not limit the children to quiet, meditative experiences. For example, you and the children can say the affirmation together while holding hands or marching to rhythmic clapping. Or you might want to try singing it to a familiar melody. The children could also write the affirmation out, illustrate it, and take turns saying it to each other. They could also make up hand motions or a dance to go with the words. Using the affirmation in stories that the children can act out is also fun. Keep trying new things, but don't hesitate to use what works again and again.

PRAYER –

When you are sitting quietly with the children and have repeated the affirmation several times, follow it with a prayer. I have included a prayer to use with each affirmation, but you may feel more comfortable with your own words. You will notice that the various prayers use different names for God. This was done to encourage the teacher to explore the different ways we can feel connected to the Eternal Spirit. Some children, however, may find it disturbing to repeatedly change the way they say their prayers, so find what works best and stay with it.

Instruct the children to sit with their spines straight and to concentrate at the Christ center, the point between the eyebrows. Explain to them that a straight spine helps increase receptivity, much like putting up the antenna on a radio. Concentrating at the point between the eyebrows is like addressing a letter—it helps send their prayers straight to God. When their eyes are gently closed, instruct the children to focus on a central point, slightly above eye level. Be sure they understand that crossing the eyes is *not* intended.

A special prayer place in your classroom will help create a devotional feeling. This will inspire the children to cooperate and concentrate. If you do not use an altar, there are other ways you can make prayer time feel special. Dim lights and candlelight are very helpful for creating a devotional atmosphere. It may also help to give the children a special pillow, bench, rug, or blanket to be used only at prayer time.

EXPLORING–

The activities presented here are for an age range of 6-10 years. Most activities should last approximately 15-20 minutes, and if used together, could easily fill a 60-90 minute class.

All the activities are explained in detail and can be used as presented. They are intended only as suggestions and can be easily adapted for use in other settings and for other age groups. Some activities are appropriate for more than one spiritual quality, and you may want to use them more than once. The suggested readings are books that should be available through any library. There are many other stories that you could no doubt find that also illustrate the qualities being discussed, and I urge you to do so. I have listed some additional resources in the back of the book.

UNDERSTANDING–

This section, intended for parents and teachers, includes a quotation taken directly from *Affirmations for Self-Healing* by J. Donald Walters. I strongly recommend *Affirmations for Self-Healing* as a companion book for anyone teaching these principles. The "Understanding" section also includes quotations from a variety of sources that make it abundantly clear that the spiritual values being studied are universal and do not belong to any one religion, path or people.

AFFIRMATION PICTURE–

These pictures can be copied and colored in the classroom, or used in other ways. The pictures are simple and leave room for children to complete them by adding their own ideas. You can use the pictures to generate discussions, to spark other drawing ideas, or to create puzzles, bulletin boards, games and art projects, and take-home materials. I've given suggestions for using certain pictures as part of the "Exploring" activities, but there are many possibilities beyond these.

Have you ever heard yourself admonishing a child: "Just *concentrate* and you can do it!" Chances are the response was, "I *am* concentrating!" The child was probably looking extremely tense and frustrated, anything but calm and concentrated. Yet, at another time, you may have seen that same child bent over building blocks or a drawing with such concentration that nothing else existed but the task in front of her.

The ability to concentrate comes naturally when the heart's feelings are involved. The ability to concentrate consciously on *all* we do is a learned skill. We can help our children develop this skill, and it will help them succeed in every endeavor.

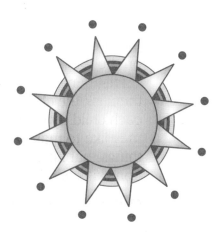

Fold

I give full attention to everything I do.

PRAYER: Lord, help me concentrate and learn to focus all my heart's energy on Thee alone.

Repro-master

Exploring Concentration

Body Work

Challenge Yourself

Concentration is required to perform difficult or dangerous physical tasks. Set up several safe challenges for the children to try. Examples might be: threading a tapestry needle with heavy thread, walking across the room balancing dried beans on a paint stick, balancing a stack of paper cups on your head, walking backwards on a line drawn or taped on the floor.

First demonstrate the tasks with an obvious lack of concentration and then ask the children how to improve on what you've shown them. Let each child try each task, without competing against one another. You may like to make a list of things that seem to help concentration and things that hinder it. Discuss what kinds of jobs require great concentration skills and how people train their bodies to focus energy.

Materials needed: tapestry needle, heavy thread, dried beans, paint stir sticks (available at paint stores), paper cups, masking tape

Creation Station

Make Your Own Game

There are many *concentration* or *memory* games available to buy. The game is played by turning over two cards at a time. Each player must remember where the cards are, and try to make a match.

You can make a set of concentration cards that have spiritual images on them, such as saints or angels, or Jesus in various poses. You can also use the affirmation pictures in this book. Copy the smaller versions that are on the TITLE pages, or use the large pages and shrink them to any size you like. You can change the difficulty level of the game by changing the number of different images and the number of repeated images. After copying the pictures, attach them to lightweight cardboard using laminating plastic or clear self-adhesive paper.

Play by traditional rules or make up your own rules concerning the number of cards that must match, time limits or number of helps each player receives. Discuss how mental concentration may be different from concentrating on a physical task. Physical skill can be increased with practice. Can mental skill benefit from practice also?

Materials needed: photocopier, lightweight cardboard, laminating plastic or clear self-adhesive paper, ten to twenty images or designs to copy

Exploring Concentration

Music

Use Music

Singing in rounds requires great concentration and can be great fun. Start with two groups of singers and work up to three or four. Sing a traditional round, such as "Row, Row, Row Your Boat," or try a more spiritual theme such as "Give Me a Light" from the *I Came From Joy!* music recording. After singing, talk about how it felt to concentrate on the parts; was it fun to be challenged? Is it easier to concentrate while singing a familiar song, or a new one? Why do you think that is?

Be Free, Inside from the *I Came From Joy!* music recording has a clapping rhythm that is a challenge and requires concentration to do correctly.

Materials needed: *I Came From Joy!* music recording, or other music appropriate for rounds

Tell Stories

Book Shelf

Bright Star, by Gary Crew and Anne Spudvilas
Could you concentrate well enough to find one small comet in the night sky, using only a small marine telescope and the technology available over one hundred years ago? John Tebbutt, a real astronomer, did so in 1861. In this story, a young girl meets a famous astronomer and longs to study the heavens as he does. Discuss how difficult it would be for a young girl in rural 19th century Australia to meet that goal. What sort of distractions and obstacles would she encounter? The image of a telescope and magnifying lenses is a perfect one for a lesson on concentration.

Supergrandpa, by David M. Schwartz
The judges said he was too old and weak, and his family didn't think he could do it either. But Gustaf wanted to ride in the "Tour of Sweden" bicycle race. It would be over one thousand miles, involve many days of riding, and require great concentration and perseverance, but that sounded like fun to sixty-six year old Gustaf. Based on a true event, this is a charming and absorbing story for everyone.

The Art Lesson, by Tomie dePaola
How does a child become a great artist? By drawing, drawing, and more drawing. Tomie never gets distracted from his goal.

The Tortoise and the Hare, by Aesop
The rabbit does not concentrate on the race and loses to the single-minded tortoise. One source for this classic is *The Children's Aesop*, by Stephanie Calmenson.

Understanding Concentration

Understand

Concentration is the secret of success in every undertaking. Without concentration, thoughts, energy, inspiration, purpose — all one's inner forces — become scattered. Concentration is the calm focus of one's full attention on the purpose at hand. Concentration means more than mental effort: It means channeling your heart's feelings, your faith, and your deep aspirations, into whatever you are doing. In that way, even the little things in life can become rich with meaning.

Concentration should not involve mental strain. When you really want something, it is difficult not to think about it. Concentrate with interest on whatever you do, and you will find yourself absorbed in it.

J. Donald Walters
Affirmations for Self-Healing

 The intellects of those who lack fixity of spiritual purpose are inconstant, their interests endlessly ramified.
Bhagavad Gita 2:41

 You can't dance at two weddings at one time.
Yiddish proverb

 To the person who seizes two things, one always slips from his grasp!
Swahili (African) proverb

I give full attention to everything I do.

There is a belief held by many, that saints are unique individuals chosen by God, which explains why they have such strong feelings of devotion. The truth is, saints and other devotees have chosen God, above all else. A saint recognizes the divine presence and concentrates all the heart's feelings into a single minded pursuit of God realization, or union with that presence.

We can't teach a child to feel devotion, but devotion can be learned. We can show our children signs of God's love in every day experiences. We can also help children explore their relationship with Spirit and encourage them to find the expression or form that speaks to their heart. Once one becomes aware of Divine Mother's loving presence, the tiny ember of devotion which exists within every soul, will burst into a bright flame in loving response.

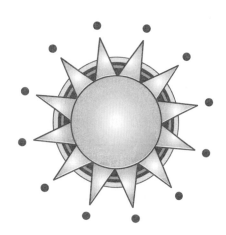

Fold

Lord, I am Thy child.

PRAYER: Heavenly Father, Divine Mother, help me grow in my love for Thee.

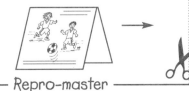

— Repro-master —

Quiet Fun

Sensing Devotion

Withdrawing from the external senses into meditation and prayer is one way to find devotion within. We can also experience the love of the divine *through* our senses and nurture our natural devotion by consciously acknowledging the divine presence all around us.

Make five flashcards with simple pictures representing each of the five senses; eyes for vision, ears for sound, hand for touch, mouth for taste, nose for smell. Describe how you might experience God through each one: we hear the sound of Aum or Eternal Spirit in the sound of the ocean, we can taste the sweetness of Divine Mother in a juicy apple, etc. Then encourage the children to give their own examples as you hold up the flashcards.

Help the discussion with questions like, "What would you miss the most if you could no longer see?" "What kind of sound makes you feel safe?" Provide paper and crayons and let everyone draw something that helps them feel God is near.

Materials needed: five flashcards or pictures representing each sense

Body Work

Sniff it Out

Using several differently scented votive candles, challenge the children to sniff out a particular scent. Place an assortment of candles on a table at the far end of the room. Place an assortment of matching candles where you and the children are sitting. Let each child take a turn being blindfolded (so the color of the candle is not a factor) and picking a candle to smell. Then let him go to the table of candles and find one with the same scent. If you have enough candles, you could have several children sniffing out candles at the same time.

Discuss how some animals have keen noses and can be trained to sniff luggage at an airport and find drugs, and how some dogs are used in finding people that are lost, simply by sniffing. Could we develop a *heart* sense that could "sniff out" God's presence? Spirit is everywhere, but seems to be very well hidden sometimes. Could we learn to detect Spirit everywhere, with practice? What would be a good name for that sixth sense?

Materials needed: variety of scented candles, blindfold

Exploring Devotion

Explore Rituals and Chants

Spiritual ceremonies and rituals are used in every religion to awaken devotion. All the senses are used to open the heart and create memories that can be drawn on at other times. Help children create memories of devotional moments by providing the setting and opportunity. A special altar for ritual ceremonies and prayer is helpful, but you can also create a devotional atmosphere in other settings using simple props.

Use the candles from the last activity; add pictures of saints, incense, prayer rugs or blankets, prayer beads, a bell or gong, flowers, and other treasures from nature. You can use familiar items from your church or setting, and also explore other spiritual paths and traditions that may be new to the children.

Chanting is used in many cultures to express and strengthen devotion. Four very different kinds of chants are: Tibetan chants, Gregorian chants, Indian chants, Native American chants. Try sharing different selections with your children.

Let the children explore the items you have; discuss how rituals can open the heart and awaken devotion. Play a chanting tape quietly. After a while, have the children sit and chant with the tape. Gradually turn the music down until you are whispering/singing, then end with a few moments of silence. Say the prayer and affirmation together.

Materials needed: spiritual objects, chanting music, **You Fill My Heart with Music**, from *I Came From Joy!* music recording

Tell Stories

In God's Name, by S. Sasso
This brightly colored picture book explores the many ways that we relate to God, and the names we can use for God.

Our Lady of Guadalupe, by Tomie dePaola
This story of a poor peasant's vision of Mary is told with dePaola's characteristic simplicity and feeling. Based on actual events, the sweetness of this man's devotion will inspire any reader.

Sacred Places, by Jane Yolen
Twelve sacred places of twelve spiritual paths are described in poetry. Even young children can feel the magic of these places if you pick out just a few to share. Let them talk about what makes a place feel special. Explain how devotional energy can accumulate at sacred sites and can be felt by visitors who go there.

I Wanted to Know All About God, by Virginia L. Kroll
"I wondered what God does in the mornings. Then I smelled the dew on the grass at dawn." One of many simple observations of God in creation.

No good end is ever reached without devotion. No true success is achieved unless the heart's feelings are involved. Will power itself is a combination of energy and feeling, directed toward fulfillment.

In the quest for God, the unfolding of the heart's natural love, in the form of deep devotion, is the prime requisite for success. Without devotion, not a single step can be taken towards Him. Devotion is no sentiment: It is the deep longing to commune with, and know, the only Reality there is.

J. Donald Walters
Affirmations for Self-Healing

I think we would be able to live in this world more peaceably if our spirituality were to come from looking not just into infinity but very closely at the world around us — and appreciating its depth and divinity.
Thomas Moore

All I have seen teaches me to trust the Creator for all I have not seen.
Ralph Waldo Emerson

God did not say, go to the east to find wisdom, sail to the west to find justice: there where you seek, you shall find, for to Him who is everywhere present, one comes by love and not by sail.
Saint Augustine

Lord, I am Thy child.

Have you ever rehearsed some terrible crisis in your mind and worried about how you would react in that situation? Have you asked yourself, "How would I *know*, in a split second, the *right* thing to do?" How do we prepare our children to deal with the inevitable crises and difficult decisions they will face? The answer to both questions is **practice**.

Imagine trying to separate a mixture of sand and sugar. This nearly impossible task may seem trivial if you have nothing at stake, and not worth your time and attention. But practicing discrimination in all the little decisions we face will enable us to see clearly when things look impossible and there is a great deal at stake. Like an ant faced with that same pile of sand and sugar, we will be able to enjoy the sweetness God offers and leave behind the sand.

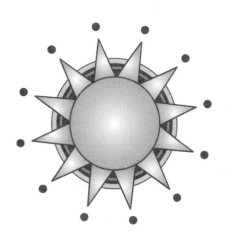

·····Fold··

I ask God to guide
all that I do.

PRAYER: Heavenly Father, I know if You guide me in all things, I will be all right.

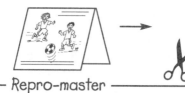

Repro-master

Body Work

Follow the Trail

Create a trail for the children to follow as they enter your classroom. Use colored yarn and start it on the floor near the door. Then take it around the room, under tables and over chairs. You can make it as difficult or easy as you like. Make it even more interesting by adding notes with directions at certain points, such as *"Jump three times before continuing."* The end point can be your altar, story circle, or a bag of treats for everyone. Try using two different colors of yarn and make two different trails. Have the children choose which one they want to follow.

Discuss how we *learn* to follow inner guidance. We don't always see what is ahead of us, and we will make mistakes, but God will always help us no matter how many mistakes we make.

Materials needed: colored yarn

Music

Use Music

The Pink Panther Theme and ***Baby Elephant Walk***, by Henry Mancini, are both lively accompaniments for activities such as *Follow the Trail* (see above).

Quiet Fun

Play "Are you sure?"

Draw two arrows, (see illustration below)), on the chalkboard or white board. Use a ruler to make sure they are the same size, and don't let the children see you draw them. Ask the children to tell you which line is longer. Then pull out the ruler and show them that they are indeed the same length, although the *illusion* is that the bottom one is longer.

You can have fun with other optical illusions you can find in game books. Use the idea of optical illusions to discuss how things are often not as they seem. We need to *discriminate* between what is true and what is not, what is really of God, and what is not.

Sample illustration

Materials needed: ruler, chalk, chalkboard

Separate Sugar and Sand

Use this as a fun demonstration. Measure approximately 1 cup of sugar and approximately 1 cup of white sand (available at craft and garden stores) and put them in different containers. Show the children the sand and the sugar. Invite them to taste the sugar and look closely at the crystals.Next pour the sand and sugar onto a tray and mix them together.

Would they want to eat the sugar now? Tell them to imagine that they are ants who want the sugar — would ants be able to take away only the sugar and leave the sand? Ask them if they can think of any way to separate the sand and sugar easily. Then bring out a clear pitcher of water and pour the mixture in. Stir until the sugar is dissolved, then let the sand settle. Discuss how higher awareness and understanding will come, if we ask God to guide our understanding and our decisions.

Materials needed: sand, sugar, containers, water, pitcher, tray

Creation Station

Draw in the Dark

Have all the children sit around a table and give everyone a piece of blank paper and one crayon or marker. Tell them you are going to give them instructions on what to draw. Then turn out the lights. If it is not dark enough in your room, you may want to use blindfolds on everyone.

Give instructions for drawing a simple picture, such as, *"Draw a house in the middle of the paper. Then draw a sun in the sky. Put a flower next to the house."* Give them time to complete each part before giving the next instruction. Make it more complex for older children. Reassure them not to worry about the quality of the drawing, all the pictures will look silly. When everyone is done, turn on the lights and let them see what they did. They will enjoy comparing their pictures.

Discuss how asking for divine guidance is like holding something up to the light to see it more clearly. If we ask God for help, instead of worrying about what other people will think of us, or what would be easiest for us, we will learn to discriminate and make good choices.

Materials needed: Paper, markers or crayons, blindfolds (optional)

Tell Stories

Book Shelf

A Baker's Portrait, by Michelle Edwards
Michelin is a portrait painter with a problem. She can't see her subjects' real beauty behind all their flaws. Uncle Ferdinand, the baker, helps her see real beauty and truth.

Seven Blind Mice, by Ed Young
The ancient tale of the Blind Men and the Elephant is retold with wit and humor. Young children catch onto the mystery the mice are trying to solve and they can keep track of colors and days of the week along the way. Older children can discuss how perspective influences our judgement. Perhaps your children can write a different version of the story. *The Blind Mice and the Giraffe? Tree? Car?*

The Key into Winter, by Janet Anderson
A young girl hides the key into winter, hoping to stop the passage of time and keep her beloved grandmother alive. But was it the right decision?

Understanding Discrimination

As science judges the relative speed of any object by one constant, the speed of light, so the devotee judges the relative merit of any idea by the one constant, God. Discrimination is clear only when it relates everything to the Eternal Absolute. Thus, while the intelligence may toy with ideas endlessly, discrimination asks, "Is this wisdom? Is it of God?"

True discrimination is not even the product of reasoning. It is soul-intuition. Reasoning, even from the highest point of reference, is uncertain compared to the inspirations of superconsciousness. To discriminate clearly, meditate first. Ask God to guide your understanding.

J. Donald Walters
Affirmations for Self-Healing

He who is not shaken by anxiety during times of sorrow, nor elated during times of happiness; who is free from egoic desires and their attendant fear and anger: such an one is of steady discrimination.
Bhagavad Gita 2:56

Appearances often are deceiving.
Aesop

The Superior Man thinks of what is right; the small man thinks of what is profitable.
Confucius

I ask God to guide all that I do.

I ask God to guide
all that I do.

Every parent and teacher has had the experience of asking a child to do something, and getting a dramatic response of exaggerated exhaustion, the child moving as if he were dragging huge weights behind him. He may even ask for help, because he feels the tremendous feat of endurance you have requested is just beyond his present capabilities. But, ask this same exhausted child if he would like to visit a favorite friend, or go out for a favorite treat, the response is full of energy and enthusiasm. The difference is willingness.

Right attitude opens us to the cosmic energy that is infinite. There really is no limit to the energy available to us, we are only limited by our willingness. We need to teach our children that God is the source of all that is, and all that is Is energy. Saints and mystics have always understood that all energy comes from the One power behind and within the universe; modern science is just catching up to the idea.

· · · · · · Fold

God's energy and power are within me.

PRAYER: Infinite Lord, recharge my body, mind and soul.

 →

— Repro-master —

Body Work

Think Energetically

The thoughts, "I'm too tired," and "I can't do it," are negative affirmations that shut off the flow of divine energy. Each time these thoughts come, counter them with the affirmation, "God's energy and power are within me!" Teach the children the power of the affirmation by creating a game.

Tape a long piece of butcher paper or newsprint on the wall, floor to ceiling. Stand next to the paper with a colored marker. Have the children take turns standing near the wall and jumping up as high as they can, reaching up the wall with their hand. You mark how high they reach with the marker. Before the first round, have all the children repeat together, "I'm too tired. I can't do it." Suggest that they think about something they think is difficult to do.

After everyone has had one turn, change the affirmation and repeat, "God's energy and power are within me!" Be positive and forceful. Encourage everyone to try harder and reach higher. Use a different color marker to record the second round, and compare all the jumps. Discuss how our thoughts are actually a form of energy and negative thoughts can change the flow of energy through us.

Materials needed: butcher paper or newsprint, two colored markers

Use Music

Music

Music conveys energy in a unique way. Play active music and encourage the children to skip around and move freely. Then change to a slower rhythm and show them how to keep their feet in one place, moving only their arms and torso. Finally, play calming, peaceful music and have everyone lie down with eyes closed. Suggest they feel the music as a rock would, not moving, but still experiencing the energy that is within all creation. Suggestions for music are below.

Active: ***We Love the Animals***, by Michael Mish
Marches by John Phillip Sousa
Polka music

Slower: ***Lightly I Fly*** and ***Sing in the Meadows***
from *I Came From Joy!* music recording.
The Blue Danube, by Strauss

Calming: ***The Mystic Harp***, by Derek Bell and Donald Walters
Selections by Steven Halpern
Baroque pieces by Bach, Mozart

Exploring Energy

Creation Station

Make a Picture

Copy the affirmation picture for each of the children. Have them cut it apart and arrange the pictures from the activity requiring the least energy, to that which requires the most. Provide other paper they can glue the pictures onto. They could glue each picture on a separate page and draw other activities that are similar in energy.

Perhaps they think the answer to the order of the pictures is obvious. Encourage some discussion with questions. How would the energy be different in each activity? Would the energy feel different in a team effort, such as soccer, and an individual effort, such as the mountain climber? Do prayer and meditation require a little energy, or a lot? Does great physical strength mean great energy and limited physical strength mean limited energy? Why do we sometimes wake up feeling tired, even though we slept all night? What kinds of things make you feel more energetic?

Materials needed: scissors, paper, glue, crayons, markers

Tell Stories

Book Shelf

When the Wind Stops, by Charlotte Zolotow
A thoughtful mother reassures her son that nothing ever ends, it begins again in another place or in a different way. Illustrated with warm paintings on wood, it is a lovely way to introduce the idea of the divine energy in all creation that cannot disappear, it can only change or be expressed in a different way.

The Eagle's Song, by Kristina Rodanas
An eagle-man and his wise eagle-mother teach a Native American tribe of the northwest how they can grow together as a community, sharing the energy of the earth and her creatures. They learn how to use drums and dancing to bring life and joy to their existence in the forest by the sea.

Days with Frog and Toad, by Arnold Lobel
"Tomorrow" and "The Kite" in this selection of stories show Frog and Toad learning lessons about energy and willingness.

The Story of Jumping Mouse, by Jonathan Steptoe
The mouse conquers unbelievable obstacles to reach his goal with his indomitable energy and perseverance in this Native American tale.

Understand

Energy is ours not when we hoard our strength, but when we devote it willingly, joyously toward the attainment of that in which we deeply believe. Faith and energy go hand in hand. If you have deep faith in what you are doing, you can move mountains. Energy is always highest when one's cause is just. The greater one's faith, the greater his will power. And the greater his will power, the greater his flow of energy.

J. Donald Walters
Affirmations for Self-Healing

The hand of God is full, and the flow of disbursal day and night does not diminish that.

The Prophet Mohammed

It is thy very energy of thought
Which keeps thee from thy God.

Cardinal John Henry Newman

God's energy and power are within me.

God's energy and power
are within me.

We have to comfort our children and reassure them that God does not want them to be hurt. The Creator always loves us. We are supposed to act as messengers for His love in the world, but often we mess up the message. Like the old game of telephone, where a message is passed along and completely mixed up by the time it reaches the end of the line; we mix up God's message with our own desires, confusions, and misunderstandings and end up hurting one another. Then we must forgive.

Getting children to say the words "I forgive you" is not enough. True forgiveness is inward and will actually remove the hurts we have from our hearts, like pulling ugly weeds in a beautiful garden. Forgiving is not simply a gift we give someone who has wronged us either; it is a step in our own spiritual growth that will enable our hearts to blossom as intended.

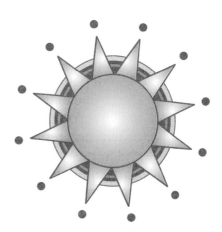

····· Fold ·

I forgive all hurts and give them to God.

PRAYER: Make me strong in Your love, God.

Repro-master

Body Work

Play "The Gardener"

Mark off a corner of the room, or have everyone sit in a large circle. Explain that everyone will have a turn being the gardener. The gardener must wear a blindfold and take a flower (see the craft activity) to *plant* in the circle, then *remove* a weed, and *find* the gardener's gloves before leaving the circle again.

Scatter crumpled pieces of paper around the circle to be the weeds. Place a pair of garden gloves in the circle, either together or separately. Use artificial flowers to plant in the circle, or make them in the craft activity. You can use enough weeds for everyone to pick, or use only one or two and replace them each time. Make it more challenging for older children by enlarging the circle or giving them a time limit. Discuss how forgiveness is like pulling weeds, it gives the blossoms of kindness and understanding a chance to grow.

Materials needed: blindfold, gloves, crumpled paper, artificial flowers, timer

Play "Telephone"

Sit in a circle and explain that you will start a message travelling around the circle by whispering it to the player to the left. Each player must pass along the message by whispering it only once to the next player, until it is carried back to you. Then the original message is revealed, and the message that was received is compared. Explain that the point of the game is to hear how the message can be mixed up, even when we try to listen and pass it on correctly. It is not an attempt to deliberately confuse or trick anyone.

If the affirmation for the lesson has not been shared yet, that would be a good message to use. Otherwise, make up something simple, geared to the age of the players. Discuss how misunderstandings cause confusion and hurt feelings. Explain how the divine message of love and cooperation is frequently mixed up when people don't listen well, or mix it up with what they want instead.

Use Music

Music

(sing to the tune ***The Wheels on the Bus***)
The joy in your heart can grow and grow
(start in squatting position)
grow and grow (stand up part way)
grow and grow (stand all the way up)
The joy in your heart can grow and grow (hands over head)
Didn't you know? (arms outstretched, hands open)
Sing additional verses: The *light*, *love*, *smile*, *flowers* in your heart can grow...

Go with Love, from *I Came From Joy!* music recording.

Creation Station

Create a Flower

Punch two pencil size holes, about one half inch apart, in the center of a saucer size paper plate. Bend a long chenille stem in half and push each end through one of the holes. Pull the two ends through to the back of the plate and wrap them around a pencil. Secure the ends of the chenille stems tightly around the pencil, keeping the pencil flat against the plate, pointing downward to become the flower stem. Wrap another chenille stem around the pencil to completely cover it.

Before assembling their flowers, older children can cut petals or glue leaves on. Younger children can color their plates. Inspire the children with pictures of gardens and flowers. Encourage them to think about someone they might forgive while making their flowers. Perhaps they have a sibling who has bothered them, or a friend at school who hurt their feelings.

Materials needed: paper plates, pencils, chenille stems, hole punch, crayons

Tell Stories

Book Shelf

St. Jerome and the Lion, by Margaret Hodges
St. Jerome removes a thorn from the lion's paw and the lion is adopted into the monastery. What happens next teaches everyone about forgiveness. This is a good story to read with participation from the children. Have them make sounds and/or motions for each character. Such as "*Rrroar*" for the lion, "*Woof*" for the dog, "*Eee-aaw*" for the donkey, "*Amen*" for St. Jerome.

The Gardener, by Sarah Stewart
The young girl in this story lives during the depression years in 1930s America, with few outward reasons to be happy. She touches everyone she meets with her sunny disposition, her ability to forgive those with less cheerful attitudes and her almost magical ability to grow flowers anywhere.

Good News, by Barbara Brenner (A Bank Street Ready-to-Read book)
Canada Goose is going to hatch her eggs soon, but by the time all her friends pass along the good news, the story has changed quite a bit and everyone is very worried. A good story to illustrate the "telephone" game.

Joseph and His Magnificent Coat of Many Colors, by Marcia Williams
This Old Testament story about young Joseph's fate and how he forgives his brothers is retold with bright colors and humor. You will find the original in Genesis 37–45.

Understanding Forgiveness

Understand

Forgiveness is the sword of victory! When we forgive those who seek to hurt us, we rob them of their very power to do us harm. Better still, if they respond with love, they will unite their strength to ours, and so our strength becomes doubled.

But forgiveness should not be given primarily for its effect on others, but rather for the freedom it affirms in our own hearts. Let no outward circumstance condition your inner happiness. Be not pleased merely when man is pleased. Be pleased, rather, when you feel God's pleasure in your heart.

J. Donald Walters
Affirmations for Self-Healing

Anger is a weed, hate is the tree.
Saint Augustine

Forgive us our trespasses,
as we forgive those who
trespass against us.
The Lord's Prayer, Matthew 6:12

The Infinite Goodness has such
wide arms that it takes whatever
turns to it.
Meister Eckhart

I forgive all hurts and give them to God.

"POOF!" was one response when I asked the class, "What would happen if God forgot about us for a single moment?" She was right. We are all a part of God's dream, or consciousness, and we wouldn't be here if God stopped being conscious of us.

We may have trouble remembering someone's name, or where we left the car keys, but we have to reassure our children that God is Eternal Spirit and does not have the same shortcomings. The Spirit of God exists within every atom of creation and therefore cannot "forget" any part of it. Because that Spirit is within each one of us, God is always nearer to us than even our dearest friends.

Difficult times are not a sign that God has forgotten us; they are a sign that we may be forgetting God's presence in our lives. God remembrance is a habit we can develop. As we do, we will find ever-increasing joy and comfort in the presence of our constant companion.

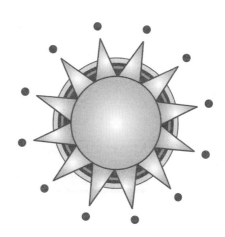

·········· Fold ··

I will remember God, as God remembers me.

TODAY
PLAY WITH GOD
EAT WITH GOD
READ WITH GOD

Repro-master

PRAYER: Dearest Friend, whether I am awake or asleep, may You always be in my thoughts.

Exploring God Remembrance

Give God a Moment

Use a kitchen timer, or the alarm on your watch, to remind your class to "Give God a Moment." Set the timer to go off several times during class, during your other activities. When the timer sounds, stop the activity and give that moment to God. Say a short prayer, have a moment of silence, or have the whole class say the affirmation together. Make it fun and energetic by saying the affirmation differently each time (*whispering, with clapping, while holding hands, or to the tune of a familiar melody*). Encourage the children to try giving God a moment at home, in the midst of their busy days.

Materials needed: timer

Test Your Memory

Gather ten to twenty small items and place them on a tray or table where everyone can see them. (If you have a large group you may want to break into teams and set up more than one game.) Use small toys, a paper clip, a crayon, and other things that are readily available in your setting.

Let all the children look carefully; then tell them to turn around and close their eyes. Remove one item from the tray and hide it in your hand. Tell them to turn around and tell you which item is missing. Let everyone have a turn choosing an item to remove. Discuss how God never forgets any of us. Even if we move, or cut our hair, or change our name, our Divine Friend is always aware of who we are and where we are and never forgets to love us.

Materials needed: 10–20 small objects

Do What I Do

Stand in a circle. You start the game by performing a simple action, like stretching your arms to the ceiling, or clapping three times. The player next to you copies your movement and adds one of his own. The next player must perform both actions and adds another. Each player adds another action and must remember all previous players' actions also. This game gets more difficult as you go along, so you may want younger players to go first. Isn't it amazing that our Divine Mother knows what each of us is doing, all the time?

Use Music

You Fill My Heart with Music from *I Came From Joy!* music recording The words of this song only refer to God as You and Thee. It leaves room for visualizing the Divine in any form.

Exploring God Remembrance

Creation Station

Create a Calendar

Make copies of a one month calendar for each child in the class. Give each child two stickers for each day of the month. They may put a sticker on the calendar for every day they know God thought about them. They may put a second sticker on each day they shared their thoughts with God. Let them decorate a frame, or create a calendar for the entire year, as a New Year project.

Materials needed: assortment of small stickers, calendars

Book Shelf

Tell Stories

Sequence Story At the beginning of class tell a simple sequence story, then enjoy your other activities. At the end of class ask the children if they remember the order of events in the story you told them earlier. Use a book if you can find a simple story that will work, or make up one. Example: *Yesterday I had a busy day. First, I had to go to the store to buy juice. Then I stopped at the gas station. After that, I went to meet my friend for lunch. When I got home, I walked my dog, then fed my bird, and played with my cat. I ate dinner and played cards before bed.*

For younger children, you could make cue cards with pictures of each event, or a key word. Mix them up and let them put them in the correct order. Discuss how our brains can keep memories a long time, but that we forget information if we don't think we'll need it later, or if it doesn't have emotional meaning. God becomes a Divine Friend that we never forget, *if we make Him important in our hearts.*

The Greatest Treasure, by Demi
 A rich man and a poor man learn to quiet the desire for material riches and express their inner joy through music. Explain to the children that the music represents Spirit in this story and anytime we are completely preoccupied with the things of this world, we are not experiencing our spirit or expressing the Infinite Spirit.

Stories Jesus Told, by Nick Butterworth and Mick Inkpen
In this collection is a humorous and meaningful retelling of the parable "The Pearl of Great Price."

The Broken Tusk, Stories of the Hindu God Ganesha
This collection of short stories provides a nice introduction to characters in Hindu mythology, centering on the figure of Ganesha. "The Old Young Woman and Her Songs" tells of a young beautiful woman who trades her youth and beauty for a life of service and devotion.

Understand

To remember God means not only to think of Him constantly, but also to realize that finding Him is an act of remembrance truly. For it is from Him that we have come. When the clouds of delusion evaporate from our minds, what will be left is what was there always, hidden behind the clouds: the blazing sun of divine consciousness!

One should not strain, nor reach outward mentally, to think of God. Know that He has been yours always — nearer than your nearest thoughts and feelings, nearer than the very prayers you offer Him! Think not merely *about* Him: Think *to* Him. Share with Him your passing feelings, your idlest fancy. Talk *with* Him. Practice His presence — at first, perhaps, for minutes a day, then for hours, and then all the time.

J. Donald Walters
Affirmations for Self-Healing

One who beholds My presence everywhere, And all things dwelling equally in Me, He never loses loving sight of Me, Nor I of him, through all eternity.

Bhagavad Gita 6:30

The purpose of this ritual prayer is not that you should stand and bow and prostrate yourself all day long. Its purpose is that you should possess continuously that spiritual state which appears to you in prayer: Whether asleep or awake, writing or reading, in all your states you should never be empty of the remembrance of God.

Jalal al-Din Rumi

I will remember God, as God remembers me.

TODAY
PLAY WITH GOD
EAT WITH GOD
READ WITH GOD

There is a legend about a man who wanted the gratitude and admiration of Saint Patrick, so he gave a large amount of meat to the church to distribute to the poor. To the wealthy man's dismay, Saint Patrick responded with only two unfamiliar words, "Deo Gratias." The man gave two more large portions of meat in the hopes of getting a response that equaled his generous gift. Twice again, Saint Patrick uttered only the words, "Deo Gratias."

When the man angrily confronted the saint and demanded proper gratitude for the large amount of food he had sacrificed for the poor, Saint Patrick calmly told him that those two simple words were greater than all the food that was given. To prove the point, he placed the meat on one side of a large scale and placed a piece of parchment, with the words "Deo Gratias" written, on the other side of the scale. The wealthy man was stunned to see the scale tip in favor of the paper, not the heavy meat. He learned his lesson about gratitude and about giving with a sincere heart. He also learned that "Deo Gratias" means "Thanks be to God."

Repro-master

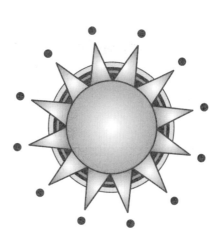

---- Fold

I give thanks to every giver, and to God for every gift.

PRAYER: Lord, thank you for this moment and all that it holds.

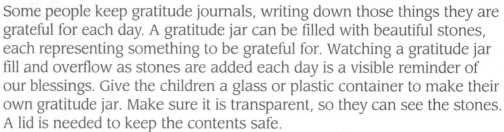

Saint Patrick was teaching a lesson and did not mean for us to forget the giver in favor of thanking only God for our gifts. We can teach our children that all things come from God, the Infinite Source of All That Is, and God uses the generous hearts of others to share the abundance of the universe with us.

Make a Gratitude Jar

Creation Station

Some people keep gratitude journals, writing down those things they are grateful for each day. A gratitude jar can be filled with beautiful stones, each representing something to be grateful for. Watching a gratitude jar fill and overflow as stones are added each day is a visible reminder of our blessings. Give the children a glass or plastic container to make their own gratitude jar. Make sure it is transparent, so they can see the stones. A lid is needed to keep the contents safe.

Large stick-on labels or nametags can be decorated with their name and placed on their jar. Provide stickers, permanent markers, fabric and paper scraps to decorate with. Give each child a small supply of smooth stones or marbles to start off with, then encourage them to add their own. It makes it more interesting if a variety of items are used, such as craft jewels, seashells, buttons, and charms.

After everyone is done, start them off by letting them share what they are grateful for and put stones in their jar. If the children think about what they are grateful for every day and place a stone in the jar, it will quickly fill up. Encourage them to keep it in a visible place so they can look at it frequently. Keep one in your classroom to use and serve as a gratitude reminder.

Materials needed: transparent jar, stickers, markers, smooth stones or marbles.

Play "The A Game"

Body Work

This game uses three cube-shaped boxes to guide the actions. One box is labeled with actions on each side of the cube (skip, hop on one foot, crawl, dance with partner, etc). The second box is labeled with attitudes on each side (like a...robot, like a...butterfly, like a...mother holding a baby, etc). The third box is labeled with directions for saying the affirmation together (whispering, singing, very slowly, silently, mouse voice, lion voice, etc.).

Start out in a circle and have two children toss the first two boxes in the center. Follow the directions that are on the top side of the cube, and perform the action with the right attitude. Then a third player may toss the affirmation box and lead everyone in the affirmation according to the instructions. Vary the game by telling the children they must travel to different spots in the room with the designated action before tossing the next box, or make it a relay with each player taking turns performing an action/attitude/affirmation.

Materials needed: three cube shape cardboard boxes (available at post offices)

Say Grace

Saying grace before meals is a traditional way to express gratitude. This is a classic for children:

> *Oh, the Lord is good to me.*
> *And so I thank the Lord,*
> *For giving me the things I need,*
> *the sun and the rain and the appleseed.*
> *The Lord is good to me.*

Teach the grace and then serve a snack of apple juice, apple slices, or apple cookies. Read the Johnny Appleseed story below.

Use Music

Say Thank You!, *I Came From Joy!* music recording.
This song will have the children imitating animals and joining in the *Thank You!* chorus.

Tell Stories

Morning Has Broken, by Eleanor Farjeon
The popular song recorded by Cat Stevens was originally a hymn for children. The pictures show us a boy and his grandfather greeting a new day with joy and gratitude for all it offers. Follow the blackbird through the pages. For more fun, find an old recording of the music to share.

It Could Always Be Worse, by Margot Zemach
The rabbi of the village helps show an unhappy man how important it is to be grateful for what one has—it could always be worse! This is a fun story with possibilities for interactive telling. Let the children make all the animal noises. You could also move the class into a smaller and smaller area during each part of the story, until you are all crowded close together. It would be a great way to illustrate the point of the story.

I Am in Charge of Celebrations, by Byrd Baylor
The Native American boy in this story has put himself in charge of celebrating every experience he is grateful for. And if you look carefully, with an open heart, there can be a celebration every moment of every day.

Johnny Appleseed, by Margaret Hodges
Here Johnny Appleseed is depicted as a real man, not a cartoon. He was a courageous pioneer who explored a great deal of unknown and uncharted territory. But his heart was at home in God. He saw God's abundance everywhere and the apples he planted were just outward signs of the blessings he shared with so many.

Understanding Gratitude

Gratitude is a way of returning energy for energy received. Only a thief takes without paying for what he gets. And one who accepts a kindness without returning gratitude, as though the kindness were his by right, demeans both the giver and himself. He demeans the giver, because by ingratitude he implies that the kindness was inspired by selfish motives. And he demeans himself, because by giving nothing in return he breaks the cycle of creativity, without which prosperity's flow, both materially and spiritually, is blocked.

Accept nothing, inwardly, for yourself, but offer everything to God. Don't let yourself be bought by others' kindnesses. Be grateful to them above all in your soul, by blessing or praying for them. Give gratitude first of all to God, from Whom alone all blessings truly come.

J. Donald Walters
Affirmations for Self-Healing

You pray in your distress and in your need: would that you might pray also in the fullness of your joy and in your days of abundance.
Kahlil Gibran

Every good gift and every perfect gift is from above,
 and cometh down from the Father of lights.
Matthew 1:17

Deo Gratias! (Thanks be to God)
Saint Patrick

I give thanks to every giver, and to God for every gift.

I give thanks to
every giver, and to
God for every gift.

Being aware of divine joy within is really an act of remembering our true nature. Beyond circumstances, beyond emotion, lies the truth that we came from joy.

Circumstances are neutral, and our reaction makes them "good" or "bad". Remembering our true nature of joy, despite circumstances, is one of our greatest challenges.

It would be difficult to convince a child of this in the midst of a crisis though. When deeply grieved or disappointed, children need comfort and unconditional love, not a lecture. The time to teach is between the emotional highs and lows that come. We also need to remember that we can't teach children what feelings to have; we just want to remind them that real happiness exists behind all the emotions.

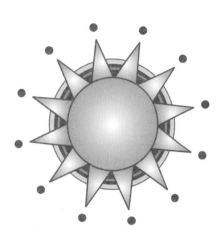

Fold

I came from God's joy, I am joy!

PRAYER: Divine Friend, help me feel Your happiness inside, always.

Repro-master

Exploring Happiness

Play "What if...?"

Prepare some common scenarios for discussion ahead of time. Examples may be: *What if you planned a fun sleepover with your best friend and he got sick and couldn't come? What if you were given a great toy and a sibling accidentally broke it? What if you planned a day at the park and the weatherman predicted a storm? What if the storm didn't come and it was sunny and warm instead?*

Ask the children to describe the feelings they might have in these circumstances or others. Don't make it a test with right or wrong answers; just explore possibilities and listen. Then ask how a young Jesus (or Saint Francis, or other saintly figure they are familiar with) might respond under the same circumstances. Why might a saint respond differently? What does a saint remember that we tend to forget?

Materials needed: prepare questions for discussion

Make Self-portraits

Use the affirmation picture with the JOY character to make Self-portraits. Use a Polaroid camera to take photos of all the children. (You just need a close-up of each face, with a smile.) After they have colored their JOY character, glue each child's photo on their character, where the face is. You will probably have to trim the pictures with scissors to fit. Let the children take a portrait home to tape on a mirror they use every day. Encourage them to repeat the affirmation to themselves whenever they look at it. Or put all the portraits together to create a joyful group picture on a bulletin board in your classroom.

Materials needed: Polaroid camera, film, crayons, markers, scissors

Use Music

Lightly I Fly and **Sing Out with Joy** from *I Came From Joy!* music recording.

Discuss the words to these songs—they give clues to ways we can transform strong emotions that can be negative and heavy, into lighter feelings of joy and true happiness. There are simple ways to help change bad moods into feelings of happiness and to transform heavy, difficult to carry burdens into the knowledge that God is JOY, always.

Clue words: *light, fly, sing, soar, above, laughter, joy, mountains, valleys*

Exploring Happiness

Body Work

Find God's Joy

Prepare cards with an emotion word written on each one. Examples: *sadness, anger, excitement, happiness, frustration, impatience, love*. On the opposite side of each card write *God's Joy*. Have one for each player. If you have to, make repeats to have enough for everyone. Read the list of words for the children before you play the game. Make sure they understand what each word means. Then explain the game to them.

   Tape a card on each child's back, with the emotion word showing, and don't let them see the card they have. Then pair off everyone with a partner. After reading their partner's card, each player must act out clues (without talking) until the partner correctly guesses the emotion. Then the other player does the same. After they guess correctly, take the card off their back and tape it to their front, with *God's Joy* face up. Discuss how God's Joy is always there, behind all the emotions we feel.

Materials needed: 3X5 cards with emotion words, tape

Book Shelf

Tell Stories

Crossing the New Bridge, by Emily Arnold McCully
The townspeople have a great deal of difficulty finding a happy person to be the first to cross the new bridge. Who is happy? Is it the richest person? The handsomest? The one with the best house, best children? It turns out to be the ones with happiness within, of course!

The Hundredth Name, by Shulamith Levey Oppenheim
An eight year old Egyptian boy is worried about his camel, who seems to always be sad. He watches his father pray five times a day, as Muslim men do; and he thinks about his father's words, "Prayer has great power, my son. It is a gift we all must use." He reaches deep within himself to pray to Allah and finds happiness for his camel and himself.

Mean Soup, by Betsy Everitt
Horace's mother shows him one way to transform strong emotions without denying his experiences or feelings. In this case it takes a big pot of boiling mean soup.

Gertrude McFuzz, by Dr. Seuss
Gertrude is a young bird who thinks she won't be happy unless she has fancy feathers. She gets into a lot of trouble trying to be the fanciest bird of all.

Understanding Happiness

Happiness is an attitude of mind, born of the simple determination to be happy under all outward circumstances. Happiness lies not in things, nor in outward attainments. It is the gold of our inner nature, buried beneath the mud of outward sense-cravings.

When you know that nothing outside you can affect you—no disappointment, no failure, no misunderstanding from others—then you will know that you have found true happiness.

J. Donald Walters
Affirmations for Self-Healing

 The greater part of our happiness or misery depends on our dispositions, and not on our circumstances. We carry the seeds of one or the other about with us in our minds wherever we go.

Martha Washington

 Think of all the beauty still left around you and be happy.

Anne Frank, Diary of a Young Girl

 There is nothing good or bad but thinking makes it so.

Shakespeare

I came from God's joy, I am joy!

If you spend time with young children, you may have noticed that you put a great deal of effort into helping them get a better view. When attending events where there are adults with young children, listen to how often you hear, "Look over here!" "You can see better from here," "I'll lift you up so you can see," "If we stand up here, you can see better," and so on. And when you see a child's face light up as he is lifted to his father's shoulders, you know why it is so important to help children see more than feet, knees and the trash on the ground. It would be silly to say that facing the reality of the dirty ground is a more valuable experience than seeing the parade passing by.

We can show our children that they have the power to look at all of life's experiences from the high ground. There is so much beauty and joy to be seen and experienced if you raise your thoughts high enough. High-mindedness is not pretending ugliness does not exist, it is celebrating the wonderful fact (Thank you God!) that there is so much more.

Repro-master

······ Fold ·

I will see goodness in everything.

PRAYER: Heavenly Father, open my eyes and heart so Your light is all I see.

Exploring High-Mindedness

Body Work

Open Wide

Show the children a scientific experiment. The lights in the room should be bright. Have a volunteer sit on a chair, facing the rest of the class. Let the other children crowd around close enough to see the volunteer's eyes. Instruct the volunteer to close her eyes and cover them with her hands, so no light gets through. Keep them covered for at least 15 seconds. Then instruct her to move her hands and open her eyes wide. Have the other children look closely and observe how her pupils constrict in the bright light.

Next, try to see if they can see the opposite effect by turning the lights out and using one dim lamp or candlelight. If you have some small mirrors, the children could practice looking at their own eyes. Explain how the pupils must open to let in more light when it is dark.

Discuss how our hearts must "open" to let in light and goodness so we can "see" more clearly. Especially when things seem dark and ugly, there is beauty and love to be seen if we are open to it. And, unlike our eyes, our hearts do not close in reaction to brightness and goodness. Experiencing the beauty our Divine Mother offers is so wonderful, we want to keep our hearts open even more.

Materials needed: small hand mirrors optional

Make a Rainbow

Before class, cut up black construction paper into small pieces, about 2X3 inches. Make 50-100 pieces, depending on your class size. Hide the pieces around the room. Make a large outline of a rainbow on your bulletin board or on the wall. Keep it simple, three stripes for three colors is enough. Cut up colored construction paper into larger pieces than the black ones and keep these in a box or bag. If the pieces are large, the rainbow will be easier to construct and the pieces may be overlapped. Three color families will work well—red/orange, yellow/green, blue/violet.

Let the children hunt for the black pieces of paper you have hidden. Each time they find one, they must give it to you and trade it for a colored piece that they may then tape to the rainbow. If your group has a large age span, limit the number of pieces the older children can find, then have them help the little ones. Or younger children could hunt first, leaving the harder to find pieces for the older children.

Rainbows are one of the natural beauties we can enjoy, if we watch out for them and look up. Discuss how dark thoughts and gloomy moods can be difficult to change, but we can consciously choose to keep our thoughts light and happy. The more we try to keep our attitude "up," the more we experience our natural joy.

Materials needed: black and three colors of construction paper, tape, scissors or paper cutter, rainbow outline

Exploring High-Mindedness

Creation Station

Wear Goodness Glasses

Wouldn't it be fun if we could give everyone "goodness" glasses that help them see God's beauty in the world? You can purchase child-size plain masks to decorate, or you can make simple "glasses" out of paper plates.

Draw lines across the plates and divide into thirds. Cut off the top and bottom thirds of the circle and use the center. Cut large eyeholes. Punch holes at the sides and use chenille stems to bend over each ear. Decorate with feathers, sequins, jewels, bright ribbon, stickers, and glitter.

Discuss how things may look different if we really had goodness glasses. Encourage the children to pretend they have goodness glasses on and see what happens.

Materials needed: masks or paper plates, scissors, glue, hole punch, chenille stems, variety of decorations

Music

Use Music

Lightly I Fly, and ***Father, Now That I Wander with Thee*** from *I Came From Joy!* music recording

High-mindedness does not just affect our consciousness, it changes our experience of life and puts us in tune with the divine consciousness. These songs reflect that reality.

Book Shelf

Tell Stories

Good Times on Grandfather Mountain, by Jacqueline Briggs Martin
Old Washburn always looks on the bright side of life. His attitude never changes, although circumstances are ever-changing. He says he whittles his way out of trouble, but the truth is, he never sees circumstances as trouble, just opportunities.

Frederick, by Leo Lionni
Frederick cheers up all the mice in the middle of winter with his memories of rainbows and summer colors.

Days with Frog and Toad, "Alone," by Arnold Lobel
Toad learns that being alone with your good thoughts can be fun.

The Way to Start a Day, by Byrd Baylor
A wonderfully uplifting book about starting each day with good thoughts.

Understanding High-Mindedness

Understand

People often speak of cynicism as the mark of realism. In fact, in a universe without any visible center, one might justifiably develop his understanding of it from any conceivable starting point. One's understanding, however, will only reflect who and what he himself is. A view from the depths lacks the perspective that can be achieved from the heights. From the mountain top, all things are seen in their true proportion.

Strive always to be a channel for high thoughts and inspirations. Never cooperate with anything petty or mean. Remember, the universe is, for each human being, both a mirror and an affirmation. One who entertains high thoughts will be, himself, ennobled.

J. Donald Walters
Affirmations for Self-Healing

Whatsoever things are true, whatsoever things are honest, whatsoever things are just, whatsoever things are pure, whatsoever things are lovely, whatsoever things are of good report; if there be any virtue, and if there be any praise, think on these things.

Phillipians 4:8

Prayer is the contemplation of the facts of life from the highest point of view.

Ralph Waldo Emerson

There is more light than can be seen through the window.

Russian proverb

I will see goodness in everything.

Most parents and teachers know that secret little twinge that pricks the conscience when their child boasts to a playmate and puffs up with pride to the point of bursting. Perhaps that twinge is fear — has our parental cheerleading created an egotist, rather than a self-confident child? Where does humility come in when self-esteem and self-confidence are valued so highly in our society?

Recognize God's power and glory with every breath, and joyfully acknowledge all that is possible through the Infinite that is our true Self. Teach children confidence in their true Self, not in the little self of I, me, mine. Cheer them on and help them to see the amazing possibilities open to them when God is the Doer, doing incredible and wonderful things through them and with them, and for them.

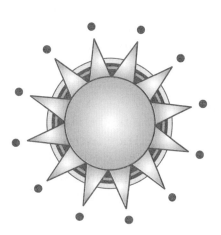

—— Fold ——

God is the Doer, and He can do it through me!

PRAYER: Dear Lord, I give You all that I am, please shine through me.

Repro-master

Creation Station

Give a Blue Ribbon

Children can make these beautiful blue ribbons to keep or to give someone in recognition of an accomplishment. Use plastic lids from margarine tubs or other containers as the base. Show the children how to use the lid as a template and then cut circles from blue paper to fit the inner side of the lids. Help them write the affirmation on the blue circle and glue it to the inside of the lid.

Cut 6-inch and 3-inch lengths of wide blue ribbon ahead of time. (It will look fancier if the ends of the ribbons are pointed.) Have the children glue the shorter pieces around the lids, sticking out like rays of the sun. Then two 6-inch pieces are glued to hang down, under the affirmation. Purchase stick-on brooch pins to attach to the backs of the plastic lids, or affix large safety pins with heavy-duty tape.

Olympic-like medallions can also be made by leaving off the hanging ribbons and cutting two slits on the edge of the plastic lid to slide a long length of ribbon through to hang around a child's neck.

Discuss how we can feel good about our accomplishments without belittling anyone. When we recognize that God is acting through us, we open ourselves to ever greater possibilities.

Materials needed: wide blue ribbon, blue paper, plastic lids, scissors, glue, brooch pins or safety pins

Quiet Fun

Wash Their Feet

Fill a large basin or bowl with warm water and place it on the floor with several towels. Have the children sit around you and take their shoes and socks off. Each child should take a turn stepping into the warm water and then onto a towel, so you may dry their feet.

As you do this, tell them the story of how Jesus washed his disciples' feet at the Last Supper (John 13: 5-17). Jesus was teaching his disciples that God resides in everyone equally, and although he was the Master, he was not above them in the eyes of God. When Peter objected, Jesus told him that to refuse was to refuse his love. Peter then asked that his hands and head be washed also.

Discuss how greater awareness does not equal greater worth, it means recognizing the One Source Of All That Is within everyone and everything.

Materials needed: basin with warm water, towels

Exploring Humility

Music

Use Music

Hallelujah chorus, from *Messiah*, by Handel
Is it possible to feel small, but uplifted and joyful at the same time?
Play any version of this classic chorus, with full orchestra, and ask the
children how they feel.

Be Free, Inside and **Father, Now That I Wander with Thee**
I Came From Joy! music recording

Book Shelf

Tell Stories

The Wise Shoemaker of Studena, by Syd Lieberman
Children love this Jewish folktale of a simple shoemaker who teaches a
proud, self-centered man and his guests an unforgettable lesson in
humility. The pictures are as bright and fun as the story.

Brother Francis and the Friendly Beasts, by Margaret Hodges
The best book for children about Saint Francis. The humble joy
expressed in the pages helps the reader feel a part of the drama. Several
of the well-known legends are told here, including the story of the first
live Christmas crèche.

Grandpappy, by Nancy White Carlstrom
Nate learns the most powerful lessons of life from his grandfather's quiet
example and simple words of wisdom. Grandpappy tells Nate, "It's okay
to feel small, you know. Small, but not alone, and dressed in glory like
the stars."

Understanding Humility

Understand

Humility is not self-deprecation; it is self-forgetfulness! It is knowing that God alone is the Doer. It is the realization that nothing in this shadow-world of appearances is all that important, except as it draws us closer to the Lord. Never tell yourself that you are sinful, or weak, or incompetent, or lazy, except as such a statement may help you to surrender joyfully to God's power. Then live by that power! Never wear the mask of false humility. Humility is self-acceptance, and self-honesty. You have a right to all power if you seek it in Infinity, and if you never hold the thought that it resides in your little self.

J. Donald Walters
Affirmations for Self-Healing

Man must do his best, of course. His best, however, will be crowned with success to the extent that he realizes that it isn't he, as a human being, who is acting, but God who is acting through him, inspiring and guiding him.

Paramhansa Yogananda

Never preen yourself that you are prideless: for pride is more invisible than an ant's footprint on a black stone in the dark of night.

Jami

A man's pride shall bring him low: but honor shall uphold the humble in spirit.

Proverbs 29:23

God is the Doer, and He can do it through me!

Think of your closest friend. Think about those times you felt so close that you communicated with a simple look or you felt like you were completing each other's unfinished thoughts. One word or phrase might spark a memory of a common experience and you laugh together without having to explain anything. The laughter you share is rooted in love and the joy of sharing life's absurdities with someone with whom you are completely comfortable.

Now think of your relationship with God. Is your relationship with the Divine filled with joyful intimate laughter also? Friendships are certainly forged over shared pain and trials, but friendships last because of shared laughter and joy. The same is true of our friendship with the Divine. Laugh with the Lord in the shared joy of true friendship. Share loving humor and laughter with your children and steer them gently back towards their center when their humor turns unkind or uncontrolled. God gave us the ability to smile, laugh, chortle, chuckle, grin and giggle. God will always share in the fun with us when our humor comes from our highest Self within.

Repro-master

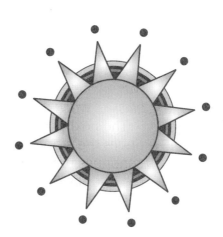

----- Fold -----

In laughter, I feel God's delight.

PRAYER: Dear Friend, make all my smiles loving smiles and all my laughter joyful prayers to Thee.

Invent a Silly Tale

Everyone in the class gets to add to a silly story in this game. Gather different items from around your classroom and put them in a paper bag. (Have at least one item for each player.) Include anything that could inspire the players to create action or characters in a silly story; a pair of glasses, a glove, jewelry, small toys, paintbrush, scissors, etc.

Pull one item out of the bag and start the story. *Once upon a time there was a young squirrel named Alvin. He was looking all over his house for his glasses, when suddenly...*

The next player in the circle takes an item out of the bag and continues the story, including the item they have, in any way they wish. Play continues until everyone has a turn. You may need to finish the story if the last player isn't able to.

Discuss how everyone has a unique contribution to make and the Lord wants to enjoy life through each one of us.

A variation would be to divide into teams and give each team 3-5 items they have to include in a story that they will tell the rest of the group. Further challenge older children by limiting them to a certain theme, such as a mystery or animal story.

Materials needed: paper bag, variety of small items from your setting

Tell Stories

***That's Good! That's Bad!*,** by Margery Cuyler
A terrifically fun tale of a boy's adventures in the jungle. Every event is accompanied by "That's good!" or "That's bad!", and the reader is kept guessing about what could possibly happen next. The humor also helps remind us that what appears to be a bad thing, could be a good thing, depending on what we need at the time.

***Hedgehog for Breakfast*,** by Ann Warren Turner
A silly misunderstanding has children giggling and groaning through this story. Are they really going to *have* hedgehog for breakfast?

***Amos Ahoy!: A Couch Adventure on Land and Sea*,** by Susan Seligson
No deep messages here, just ridiculous fun with Amos the dog on his motorized couch.

Exploring Humor

Creation Station

Make Funny People

Make a whole group of silly people for your bulletin board. Everyone sits at a table with crayons or markers within reach. Each person gets a piece of paper that has been folded into three equal sections. Tell everyone they are to draw the head of a person on the top section of the paper. You decide beforehand if you want these to be imaginary creatures or silly people. Give guidelines to inspire and guide the group.

When sufficient time has been allowed, tell everyone to fold over the top of the paper towards the back, hiding their part of the picture, and pass it to the person on their right. Then instruct everyone to draw the torso of an imaginary person on the middle section of their paper, without looking at the head that has already been drawn. Each person then folds over the middle section, hiding their drawing, and passes it to the person on their right. Everyone then draws legs on the bottom section. After everyone is finished, open up each drawing and reveal the completed silly people. Discuss how everything cannot be planned and anticipated, but the unexpected can be fun with the Divine as our companion and guide.

This can also be fun with teams and large rolls of paper. Use three tables, with a long piece of art paper at each table. Assign one team to each table to work together on drawing the head. Each team folds their picture and moves to the next table to draw a torso. Each team hides their work by folding the paper and then moves to the last table to draw legs. You'll have three drawings that everyone has contributed to.

Materials needed: paper, markers or crayons

Use Music

Music

Baroque Trumpet music by Vivaldi or other composers is fun and lively accompaniment for games and art projects.

Balloon Dance Use the Baroque music above, or any lively music that is easy to move to. Have the children pair off and give each pair a balloon. Tell them they can dance to the music any way they want, but they have to keep the balloon pressed between them and off the floor. Show them how they can stand back to back with the balloon between them, or they can each keep one hand on the balloon.

Play the music and let them try moving without letting the balloon drop. Stop the music after a minute or two, or if someone drops their balloon. Let each pair move their balloon to a new position and then play the music again. Let them try several positions, or make it harder by increasing the number in each group, and the number of balloons they use.

Understand

A good sense of humor is an effective means of keeping a sense of perspective through the trials and difficulties of life. By not taking things too seriously, one develops non-attachment.

One should not laugh too much, however, lest the mind become light, and one's view of life, superficial. Thus, one needs to achieve a sense of perspective where humor itself is concerned. The best way to do so is to share one's laughter with God; to laugh with the sense of His joy, within. Never laugh at people, but rather with them. For humor should be kindly, not sarcastic. Laugh with pure delight, and everyone will join you in your laughter.

J. Donald Walters
Affirmations for Self-Healing

Humor is a prelude to faith and
Laughter is the beginning of prayer.
Reinhold Niebuhr

I am especially glad of the divine gift
of laughter; it has made the world
human and lovable, despite all its
pain and wrong.
W. E. B. Du Bois

Angels can fly because they take
themselves lightly.
G. K. Chesterton

The laughter of a child is the light of
the house.
Swahili (African) proverb

In laughter, I feel God's delight.

In laughter I feel
God's delight.

We want our children to have a positive self-image, yet we do a great disservice if we focus so much effort on building up self-esteem that we forget to teach them the power of honest self-examination and introspection. After introspection, however, don't leave out the next step—what to do with what is revealed.

The surest way to stop spiritual growth is to limit our identity to our mistakes and burden ourselves with guilt. Our good deeds do not define who we are either. We need to help our children remember that they are spiritual beings with unlimited potential and that God will help them grow beyond every mistake *and* every success.

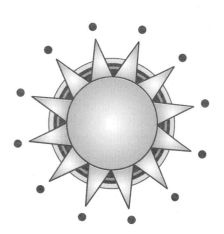

· · · · · · · · · · · · · · · Fold ·

I am God's child, and God will help me grow.

PRAYER: Divine Mother, help me to clearly see my faults and how to grow in Your love and light.

Repro-master

Exploring Introspection

Body Work

Find Your Inner Self

Demonstrate how our Inner Self is often hiding behind sands of ego and wrong action. Use a large clear crystal, prism, or glass paperweight to represent the inner Self. Cover it in a bowl of wet sand. Let your hands play in the sand as you talk about how God can help us find the treasure of our true inner Self within. Then pull out the crystal, wash it off and let the children see how beautiful it is. Show them how the light can now brightly shine through it.

You can expand this idea for a group activity. Purchase craft jewels, or clear beads for the entire class. Hide them in a large basin of sand and let the children hunt for them, or give each child a bowl with one jewel to find. Sand works well, especially if you can go outside, but rice is an alternative for inside clean up.

The children can draw pictures of themselves and glue their jewels in the center as their inner Self.

Materials needed: clear beads or craft jewels, bowls, sand or rice

Music

Use Music

Play slow-moving music and lead the children in the Caterpillar Crawl. Let everyone try crawling like a caterpillar to the music and then show them how to hook up and make one giant caterpillar. Each player places their hands on the waist of the player in front of them, forming a long chain. Show them how to stretch their arms out as far as possible, without letting go of the other player. Then tell them to spread their legs, bend their knees, and walk slowly forward. You hook up to the front of the line and put your arms up in the air, to make the antennae. Try getting the children to scrunch up close and then stretch out, like a caterpillar moves.

Change the music to a faster piece and pass out scarves to everyone. Now you all are butterflies and can move freely about the room to the rhythm of the music. Remind the children that a caterpillar doesn't worry about whether it can be a butterfly, it just becomes one naturally.

Materials needed: slow, uplifting music such as, ***Nightingale*** from the *I Came From Joy!* music recording or ***Jesu, Joy of Man's Desiring*** by Bach; and faster moving music such as ***Waltz of the Flowers*** by Tchaikovsky; Assorted scarves (inexpensive scarves can be found in second-hand shops and thrift stores.)

Creation Station

Make a Sweet Butterfly

Transform a roll of candy, a piece of paper and a chenille stem into a beautiful butterfly. Older children can cut the paper into complex designs, younger children just fold and color. The chenille stem antennae can be added to the candy alone, to make a caterpillar.

Fold an 8.5 X 11-inch paper diagonally, so the two straight edges are an inch apart, and the corners form a "W" shape. (See *appendix* for picture.) Fold in half and make a crease down the middle of the "W", then open. Fold the paper the opposite way and make a crease one-inch to the left and one inch to the right of the centerfold, then open. Use the hole punch to make one hole on each side of the center line. The roll of candy sits in the centerfold to make the body and the chenille stem is pulled through the two holes to attach the wings and form the antennae.

Discuss how difficult it is to feel like a butterfly when we make mistakes. We have to try and remember that we are children of Spirit and mistakes can help us grow. Our Divine Mother will always help us realize our potential, even as She helps the caterpillar become a butterfly.

Materials needed: 8.5 X 11 colored paper, Lifesavers® candy, black chenille stems

Tell Stories

Book Shelf

I Believe in Me!, by Connie Bowen
An inspiring book to affirm a child's inner wholeness. Simple affirmations such as "I am filled with greatness" are paired with bright beautiful illustrations. Let your children pick their favorite. Show them a picture and have them write their own affirmation to go with it.

Designed by God, so I Must Be Special, by Bonnie Sosé and Character Builders for Kids

A bright, positive book for young children that teaches the five senses and that each one is a gift from God. Illustrated with child-like drawings in primary colors.

When Solomon was King, by Sheila MacGill-Callahan
This story tells of how the young Solomon, son of King David, learned a valuable lesson in compassion and courage from a wounded lioness. When he became king, he was given a ring that enabled him to communicate with all animals, and for some time he ruled with justice and mercy. He later forgot where his power came from and why he was king; his heart filled with arrogance and pride. Another lesson from the lioness helps him admit his mistake and grow in his wisdom, as we would expect King Solomon to do.

Understanding Introspection

Understand

People commonly delude themselves with easy rationalizations. "Maybe I wasn't as kind as I might have been," they'll say, "but wouldn't you have been unkind, too, if he'd treated you that way? It wasn't my fault. The fault was his." Thus, the blame for every wrong is placed at one's neighbor's door.

Introspection means to behold oneself from a center of inner calmness, without the slightest mental bias, open to what may be wrong in oneself — not excusing it, but not condemning, either. Introspection means referring what one sees to the superconscious mind, and detachedly accepting guidance, when it comes.

J. Donald Walters
Affirmations for Self-Healing

Do you wish for kindness? be kind;
Do you ask for truth? be true.
What you give of yourself, you find;
Your world is a reflex of you.

Look without. What you are,
doubt it not,
You will see, you will feel in another;
Be you charity stainless of blot,
And how loving the heart of your
brother!

From "Do Unto Others",
The Kindergarten Speaker,
by Florence Underwood Colt, 1900

It is easy to see the faults of others,
but difficult to see one's own faults.
One shows the faults of others like
chaff winnowed in the wind, but one
conceals one's own faults as a cun-
ning gambler conceals his dice.
Buddha, The Dhammapada

Confucius said, "When you see a
good man, try to emulate his
example, and when you see a bad
man, search yourself for his faults."
Confucius

I am God's child,
and God will help
me grow.

Exposure to people of different cultures, ages, interests, and backgrounds can help children develop feelings of acceptance and kindness for others. But there has to be more to create a genuine connection with others—there has to be a deep awareness of the universal Divine Presence within.

If that awareness is not there, then you'll have a well-educated person with knowledge of other cultures, who still feels alone in the world. If that awareness *is* there, then even if you never leave the neighborhood, the whole world is your home and the human race, your family.

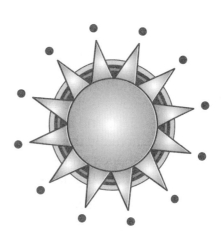

Fold

The whole world is home, and we are God's family.

PRAYER: Divine Mother, help me see that kindness attracts kindness, and Thy love.

Repro-master

Quiet Fun

See One Light

Prepare a demonstration before class. Using a single-hole paper punch, make multiple holes in a paper lunch bag. You may create a design or a random pattern. Make lots of holes all around the bag. Have a votive candle and holder ready to use.

During class, turn off the lights, put the candle in the candleholder, light the candle, and place it in the bottom of the bag. (Don't leave it unattended or let the children play with it.) Explain how each of the holes is like one of us, and the light that shines through is the light of God. The lights we see on the walls and floor look separate, but it is actually the *same* light shining in each one. The holes could be different shapes and sizes, but the light shining through would still be the same. Adapt this idea in the craft activity below.

Materials needed: votive candle and holder, paper bag, single hole punch

Make One Light Flashlights

Let the children create their own paper bag candle holders, but demonstrate how it can be used with a flashlight instead. Carefully gather the edges of the bag to fit the flashlight. Hold it there with your hand, or tape it in place. A bag can simply be set over a lantern style flashlight that sits on a table.

Let the children use hole punchers to make holes in their sack, or show them how to pinch the paper and cut small holes with scissors. The holes won't be round, but the pattern of light will be even more interesting. If you are prepared with several flashlights, they can try them out before taking them home.

Materials needed: small paper bags, single hole punch, scissors, tape, flashlights

Creation Station

Create Paper People

Old fashioned paper doll chains, where each figure is connected to the next, can be used to teach our connection to others also. See *appendix* (page 166) for sample patterns, or make one of your own using stencils or cookie cutters. Show the children how to outline the shape on the edge of a long piece of paper. Use this shape as a guide to accordion fold the paper to the right side. Make sure the figure is touching the folds on both sides. Cut out the figure, leaving a portion on the folds uncut, so when opened, it will be a chain. Use lightweight paper that is easy to cut when folded several times, such as wrapping paper, or shelf paper that comes on a roll. Discuss how all creation is connected on an *inner* level.

Materials needed: gift wrap or shelf paper, scissors, patterns, pencils

Exploring Kindness

Body Work

Play "Connections"

Choose some music to play and tell the children they may dance to the music in whatever way they like. When the music stops, everyone must stop and stand in one spot. Take the ball of yarn and wrap it around your ankle and then roll it to a player close to you. That player must wrap the yarn around their ankle and hold the ball of yarn.

Play the music again and let the children dance around. Players that are attached to the yarn can only move their upper bodies while keeping their feet still. When the music stops, everyone stops moving and the player with the yarn rolls it to another player who is now connected in the same way. Keep playing until everyone is connected by the yarn. To finish the game, play the music and see how long it takes to roll the yarn back to each player in turn and disconnect everyone.

Discuss the connection we have with others that can never be broken. We all come from the same Source.

Materials needed: music, ball of yarn

Music

Use Music

Handel's **Water Music Suite** is lively enough to dance to, or try some fun Big Band music from the 1940s to use in the activity above.
All the World Is My Friend and **Go With Love**, from *I Came From Joy!* music recording.

Book Shelf

Tell Stories

A Guest Is a Guest, by John Himmelman
This kind-hearted family treats everyone with the same gracious generosity. Their home is overrun by their animal guests until they figure out how to get their house back, with kindness.

Good King Wenceslaus, J. Henterly
The words to the well-known Christmas carol are here, telling the story of the kindly king. Beautiful illustrations make it a story for anytime.

The Good Samaritan Parable, Luke 10:30-37
Retold in *Parables for Children*, by Tomie dePaola, and *Stories Jesus Told*, by Nick Butterworth and Mick Inkpen.

One Hundred Is a Family, by Pam Ryan and **People**, by Benrei Huang and Peter Spier, both illustrate the oneness of the human family.

Understanding Kindness

Understand

When you can view all human beings as members of your own extended family—your brothers and sisters, mothers, fathers, and children—then you will find wherever you go that love awaits you, welcomes you! It is God who gazes back at you, when you behold Him in all!

Kindness is the recognition that all are truly our own. Kindness comes from not minding how others feel about us. It comes from the simple understanding that kindness is its own reward, worth giving out to others, because the source of so much sweetness in ourselves. For those of broad sympathies, the very universe is home!

J. Donald Walters
Affirmations for Self-Healing

I am not an Athenian or a Greek, but a citizen of the world.
Socrates

We must love others not for their human personalities, but because they are manifestations of God, Who dwells equally in all.
Paramhansa Yogananda

Master, which is the great commandment in the law? Jesus said unto him, Thou shalt love the Lord thy God with all thy heart, and with all thy soul, and with all thy mind. This is the first and great commandment. And the second is like unto it, Thou shall love thy neighbour as thyself. On these two commandments hang all the law and the prophets.
Matthew 22:36-40

My true religion is kindness.
Dalai Lama

The whole world is home, and we are God's family.

We are supposed to love everybody! are words I frequently hear from children while teaching Sunday School. The words are sometimes flung at a classmate in chastisement, or said in a solemn confessional tone, with resignation that this ideal will never be lived up to. If given the opportunity, children will go on to list the many reasons why people can be so difficult to love.

We can relieve the burden of living up to this goal of loving everybody if we understand that we are not responsible for creating love, or for passing it out in equal portions to everyone we see. We are responsible for receiving God's love and letting it flow through us at every opportunity. Leave the rest to God. Let your children know that you have to pray for help when you feel less than loving, and reassure them that our Divine Mother's love for us is constant, even though our loving feelings for others may not be.

Fold

God's love flows through me.

PRAYER: Divine Mother, fill me with Your love until it overflows to everyone I meet.

Repro-master

Let It Flow

This demonstration can be a great deal of fun in a large group. Arrange everyone in a circle, including yourself. Then give each person a small cup that is easily held in one hand. Fill a pitcher with water and fill the person's cup to the left of you. She in turn pours the water into the next person's cup, who pours it into the next person's cup, and the water is passed around the circle. As soon as the first cup is emptied, refill it from the pitcher until everyone has water and has to pass it on before receiving more. The last person can pour back into the pitcher.

Keep the water going for a while and encourage discussion. If the water represents love, what is the source? As water flows down a river, we say it flows through *channels*. Does love flow through channels also? How can we be pure channels so that love flows through easily?

Materials needed: pitcher of water, small paper or plastic cups

Make a Hug

Use a roll of butcher paper or craft paper. Roll it out on the floor and show the children that they will take turns lying on the paper, with their arms extended. The paper should extend from fingertip to fingertip, behind their shoulders. Trace around their arms and hands and cut off the length of paper, which will be as long as their "hug" would be.

On a separate piece of colored paper, let the children write the verse, or write it out for them before class. Let the children decorate their verse if they wish, and then glue it to the center of the hug. Roll up the paper hug and tie with bright ribbon. Let the children take their hug home for someone special. (*See appendix for picture.*)

Verse: *Here is a loving hug from me to you.*
I am glad God gave us hugs and God gave me you!

Materials needed: butcher or craft paper, markers, scissors, colored paper, ribbon

Tell Stories

Mama, Do You Love Me?, by Barbara M. Joosse
A young Inuit girl is reassured by her mother that she will be loved "...till the stars turn to fish in the sky."

Somebody Loves You, Mr. Hatch, by Eileen Spinelli
A simple note and box of chocolates changes a life forever.

Mother's Day Mice, by Eve Bunting
Three mice choose gifts for mother in a happy tale that exudes warmth and love.

Exploring Love

Visualize Love

Guide the children through a visualization exercise to expand their awareness of the love they may have experienced with a pet. Read this example over several times so you can lead the visualization without reading it. Speak softly, and pause after each sentence. Let the children lie on their backs and dim the lights. This exercise will take about five minutes with younger children, but could take as long as ten with older children by allowing longer pauses and a few silent moments at the end.

Inhale deeply, tense your body, then exhale forcibly and let go of all the tension. Repeat. Close your eyes. Imagine your pet is sitting in front of you. (If a child does not have a pet, tell them to follow the same steps, but imagine their best friend or someone else they love.) Picture a white light surrounding your pet and expand that light to include you. You are both bathed in the light. Feel the light glowing around you and within you and your pet. Nothing can change the connection you have with your pet. If your pet is far away, or if your pet dies, the connection and the light are still there.

Imagine expanding the light until it fills the room you are in, and it continues to grow larger than the building. Keep expanding the light until it covers the world. Now concentrate on the light in your heart. Thank God for the love that flows through you and your pet. Take a slow, deep breath, and open your eyes.

Pass It On

Get all players to form a circle. Show the children the ball that will be used in the game, and explain that they have to create new and unusual ways to pass the ball to each other. Each player's pass must be unique, but can combine moves that other players have used.

A ball small enough to hold in one hand is best, but use whatever you have available. If you don't have a ball, the game can be played with a tight ball of scrunched paper. If you can go outside, or have room to move, space out everyone and include bounces and rolls in your passes. In limited space, you can do this in a closed circle, even while sitting on chairs. Play until they run out of ideas. Discuss how everyone is a unique channel for love and although we don't *create* love, we do *express* it in our own way.

Materials needed: one small ball

Use Music

Go with Love *I Came From Joy!* music recording. A wonderfully simple song to open the heart.

I, Omar, by J. Donald Walters
Lovely instrumental music for visualization exercise.

One finds love not by being loved, but by loving. We can never know love if we try to draw others to ourselves; nor can we find it by centering our love in them. For love is infinite; it is never ours to create. We can only channel it from its source in Infinity to all whom we meet.

The more we forget ourselves in giving to others, the better we can understand what love really is. And the more we love as channels for God's love, the more we can understand that His is the one love in all the universe.

J. Donald Walters
Affirmations for Self-Healing

I am so washed in the tide of His measureless love that I seem to be below the surface of a sea and cannot touch or see or feel anything around me except its water.
Catherine of Genoa

If you would progress a long way along this road, the important thing is not to think much, but to love much. Do then whatever arouses you to love.
Teresa of Avila

Love is not an emotion that begins in us and ends in the positive response of another. Love is a divine energy that begins in God and has no end.
Eric Butterworth

God's love flows through me.

Most children understand harmful *actions* at an early age. But the idea that words and thoughts can also cause harm is a more advanced and subtle concept. Words are powerful, because they carry the energy of the thought form behind them. Thoughts alone can do harm because we don't create our own thoughts; we simply draw them from the level of consciousness to which we are attuned. Harmful thoughts mean we are allowing ourselves to sink into a lower, darker consciousness, which will only attract more darkness.

Thinking about our "bad" thoughts will not change our consciousness, we have to draw in higher thoughts that will bring light. The more we fill our hearts and minds with thoughts of blessing and harmlessness, the more light and love there will be in the world.

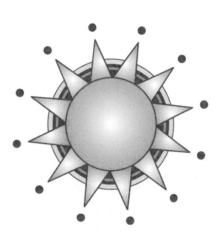

· · · · · · Fold ·

I wish only blessings for all.

PRAYER: Heavenly Friend, help me to act with blessing, speak with blessing, and think with blessing, in all circumstances.

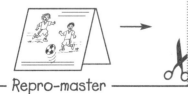

—— Repro-master ——

Speak Joyful Words

We have many words that describe positive behavior and positive thoughts. Give your children a strong happy vocabulary that will help them throughout their lifetime. Examples: *good, glad, joyful, cheerful, lighthearted, blissful, delightful, beautiful, nice, friendly, compassionate, kindly, helpful, healing.*

Let the children write their own lists, or you can write them on a white board while they call them out. Go over all the words and make sure everyone is familiar with them. You can also create a crossword puzzle, or sentences with fill in the blanks, using the words you can come up with. Ask the children to complete sentences such as: "I feel cheerful when ..." "I think it is delightful to ..." "It is helpful to ..."

Materials needed: paper or white board

Create a Collage

Children old enough to read can create word collages using their joyful word list. Bring catalogs, magazines, and junk mail for them to cut up. They may not find all their words spelled out; they may have to cut apart other words and use the letters to spell them. That will make a more interesting collage, too. Glue the words on heavy paper or cardboard, or your bulletin board.

Materials needed: scissors, glue, paper, catalogs, magazines, junk mail to cut up

Draw Blessing Pictures

If your children are too young to make collages, ask them to make a blessing picture. What do they think a blessing would look like, if they could see one? Perhaps bright and shiny like a star? or warm and fuzzy like a bunny? or colorful like a rainbow? Discuss how even our thoughts can be blessings we give to others.

Materials needed: paper, crayons, markers

Music

Use Music

All the World Is My Friend, ***Hello There, Brother Bluebell***, ***Woodland Devas***, ***Channels***, *I Came From Joy!* music recording

Blessing songs Make up a simple blessing song, or just change the words to a familiar tune. Use this song instead of the traditional birthday song in your classroom birthday celebrations. Use it to greet new children or guests. Use it to send blessings to someone leaving on a trip, or to remember someone who is absent. Help the children visualize someone they know who needs blessings, then sing the song together, after repeating the affirmation and prayer. For example: *God's blessings on you, God's blessings on you, God's blessings on (name), His love light your way.* Sing to "Happy Birthday" tune.

Body Work

Save the Eggs!

In this game, the players must save the eggs and get them back to the nest safely. Scrunch newspaper into balls to make your "eggs". Use 2–3 sheets of newspaper per egg. Scatter the eggs around the room.

Divide your group into two teams and give each team a bucket (this is the "nest") and a single paper towel. On your signal, players take turns rescuing an egg and bringing it back to the team's nest. But eggs are fragile and must be handled with care. Show the children how they must put their paper towel on the floor, place one egg in the center, and carry the egg by holding the edges of the paper towel. After all the eggs have been rescued, count how many each team has in their nest. You can also give each player a paper towel and let everyone rescue eggs at once, until all the eggs are in a nest. Time how long it takes to get all the eggs.

After you play, discuss how easy it can be to hurt others with our actions, our thoughts and our words. An attitude of non-injury means trying not to do harm in any way.

Materials needed: newspaper, paper towels, buckets

Book Shelf

Tell Stories

Bless Us All, A Child's Yearbook of Blessings, by Cynthia Rylant
Simple blessings for everyday people and everyday things are accompanied by bright paintings for every month of the year.

The Bird House, by Cynthia Rylant
A fascinating story of a frightened young girl who discovers that there are places in this world where only love and blessings exist and even the birds know they are safe from all harm.

A Fairy Went A-Marketing, by Rose Fyleman
What child wouldn't love to have a tiny mouse to run all her errands? But this fairy loves the mouse enough to let it go.

Understanding Non-Injury

Understand

Non-injury is a fundamental rule in the spiritual life. It means primarily an attitude of mind. Outwardly, one cannot avoid doing a certain amount of injury—for example, to flying insects when driving one's car. The harm one does, however, by wishing to harm others hurts not only them, but even more especially, oneself. Spiritually, a harmful attitude separates one from the harmony and oneness of life.

Non-injury, on the other hand, embraces that oneness, and is in turn sustained by it. Non-injury is a powerful force for victory, for it enlists cooperation from the very universe, where harmfulness incites endless opposition.

J. Donald Walters
Affirmations for Self-Healing

Thus, the deepest element of God's commandment to protect human life is the requirement to show reverence and love for every person and the life of every person.
Pope John Paul II

You can't love God and at the same time be unkind to your associates. You can't love Him and be full of wrath. How you behave towards others both reflects your inner consciousness and conditions it.
Paramhansa Yogananda

No one ever perfectly loved God who did not perfectly love some of His creatures in this world.
Marguerite of Navarre

I wish only
blessings
for all.

There are so many ways our children can be influenced and led in directions that are harmful. Do we really want to encourage *openness*? Shouldn't we be teaching caution and strong defenses instead? Yet, it is exactly because of all the harmful influences that it is so important to keep our hearts open to the Divine. God is always there, speaking to us in so many ways. We miss so much simply because we are not listening for that Inner Voice in our lives.

However, just as the antennae and the right frequency are important for clear radio reception, spiritual attunement and discernment are vital for clarity in spiritual receptivity.

Attunement means keeping your consciousness in the right *place*, or vibration that enables you to receive what God is offering. Spiritual practices of all kinds help our attunement. And *practice* is a key word here: this all takes practice, practice, and more practice.

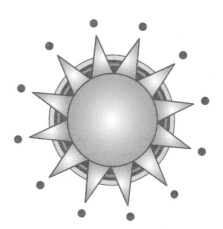

··· Fold ··

I listen for God's voice everywhere.

PRAYER: Divine Mother, help me hear Thy voice within the silence and behind every sound.

Repro-master

Listen Carefully

This simple listening game can be fun and challenging. Collect a variety of small objects in a paper bag and show them to the children. Examples: *pencil, paper clip, jewelry, erasers, small blocks or toys, hair ribbon, etc.* Try to have different sizes and textures.

Turn your back to the children and select one item from the bag, and place it in a cardboard box. The box should have a lid, be small enough to hold easily, but big enough for the item to roll around in when you shake it. Pass the box around and let each child shake it. Tell them to try and guess which item you chose. Let them all guess before you tell them the correct answer. Let the children take turns choosing and challenging everyone else.

Discuss how it takes practice to listen well. If you had not shown them the items first, would it have been harder? When they hold the box, they have additional information, such as weight and vibrations, to confirm what they are hearing. When we are trying to be open and listen with our Inner Self, we also have to pay attention to clues that guide our understanding.

Materials needed: assortment of small items, paper bag, cardboard box with lid

Create Radio G-O-D

Being receptive and open to the Divine really is like fine tuning an internal radio. Just being open to anything may get you static, or harmful vibrations you really don't want to listen to. Telling yourself God is everywhere doesn't work. You have to tune into the right vibrations. Help the children understand this subtle truth by making G-O-D radios.

Use lightweight cardboard or poster board, approximately 8.5 x 11 inches. Use pencil to outline a design of a radio and then go over it with black marker. Draw a large "speaker" in the shape of a heart. Draw a rectangular "digital" display that spells G-O-D. Fill the rest of the space with smaller rectangles and circles to represent other controls. Add an antenna with a five-pointed star at the top. Punch two holes and add string so the children can hang them around their necks. Adapt the idea and decorate boxes to look like radios. Older children can design their own with the same basic elements. Younger children could color your design. (*See appendix for an example.*)

Discuss how our heart is the receiving center, where we feel/hear God's voice. The star antenna represents the spiritual eye, where we focus our concentration. We have a choice of where we tune into. What do you want *your* internal radio to be playing?

Materials needed: poster board, markers, string, hole punch, crayons

Body Work

Open Up!

Split the children into two teams. Line up each team, facing the other, so each person is facing someone else. There should about 5 feet in between the teams. One side stands with arms folded against their chests. The other team is given a bag of cotton balls and a time limit.

As one team throws cotton balls, the other team tries to catch the cotton balls. Of course, this will be tricky, with their arms crossed. After time is up, count any cotton balls actually caught and switch sides. This could be a relay, with each player throwing ten cotton balls in turn, to one player. You may want to repeat the game, allowing the players to have arms outstretched, and then count how many more they were able to catch.

Discuss how listening for God within also means being open to possibilities. God uses channels, people and circumstances, to guide us and teach us. If we are open to possibilities, that Divine Voice can come to us in countless ways. When we close ourselves off, it simply can't get in.

Materials needed: cotton balls

Tell Stories

Book Shelf

Harvey Potter's Balloon Farm, by Jerdine Nolen
This down-to-earth, fantastical tale makes you believe anything is possible and that there could be a balloon farm just around the next corner. It also raises a fascinating question: What would you plant if you could grow a crop of anything?

The Little Painter of Sabana Grande, by Patricia Maloney Markun
What does a young artist do after spending days making paint and planning beautiful pictures, only to discover he has no paper to paint on? If he is open to new possibilities, amazing things can happen.

The Legend of the Christmas Rose, retold by Ellin Greene
This legend tells of a harsh lesson learned by a young monk, and is best for older children. A miraculous garden appears every Christmas, in the forest near the home of a poor family ostracized by the villagers. The young monk cannot accept the possibility that the garden is holy and the power of his denial destroys the garden forever. Only the Christmas rose lives on as a reminder.

Understand

Openness can be a great virtue, but only when it is exercised with discrimination. To be open to wrong ideas, or to people who would harm you, would be foolish. For it is not with openness that error can be conquered, but with love.

Openness of mind is a virtue when it is centered in the desire for the truth. Openness of heart is a virtue when it is centered in love for God. Both mind and heart, however, need filters to screen out what is not true, and what is not of God. This we can do by referring back for approval to the divine presence within whatever comes to us. We must be ever open to truth and to God, but ever closed, or at least indifferent, to error and delusion.

J. Donald Walters
Affirmations for Self-Healing

No one must forget that the Lord, as the master of the laborers in the vineyard, calls at every hour of life so as to make His holy will more precisely and explicitly known. Therefore, the fundamental and continuous attitude of the disciple should be one of vigilance and a conscious attentiveness to the voice of God.
Pope John Paul II

If we have listening ears, God speaks to us in our own language, whatever that language is.
Mohandas (Mahatma) Gandhi

God gives nothing to those who keep their arms crossed.
Bambara (African) proverb

I listen for God's voice everywhere.

Most children would probably define being patient as waiting a long time for something they want, or perhaps putting up with something unpleasant without complaining. Patience is a trait highly valued by parents and teachers, but *not* by spirited young people who live for the moment. The longer rhythms of life, and eternity, seem far removed from young children's rapid movements, rapid thoughts, rapid growth and insatiable curiosity.

In his affirmation, Donald Walters uses the ocean depths to illustrate the idea of patience. It is a metaphor that works, and can be used with children as well. The slow-moving currents in the ocean depths move in a rhythm untouched by the ever-changing surface of the sea. The eternal currents of the cosmic ocean also flow without change despite storms that blow in more superficial realities.

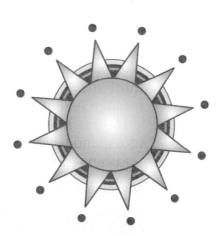

Fold

I am like the ocean deep, untouched by storm or change.

PRAYER: Lord, help me to always live in Your stillness.

— Repro-master —

Body Work

Make Waves

Use a long length of blue or green cloth. Have one child hold each end of the cloth and shake it to make "waves." Start the game with them sitting or kneeling on the floor. Have the other children try to cross over the waves. Let the children take turns being the wave makers.

Then have the children holding the cloth move a bit higher. Let the other children lie down flat on the floor, under the cloth, and try to keep quiet and still while the waves crash over them. Time how long they can be calm and quiet. Play an ocean sounds recording to make it more fun.

Discuss how circumstances are often out of our control. Patience helps us expand beyond our little self, even though circumstances keep "crashing" around us.

Materials needed: approximately 3-4 yards of blue/green cloth

Fish for Patience

Before class, cut 3x5 cards in half and write a positive word on each one. For example, *joy, happiness, love, peace, calmness, friendship, fun*. Be sure to include *patient* too! You can make multiple cards with the same words. (The children can "fish" for as many as ten cards each.) Attach a metal paper clip to each card.

Make a fishing pole by tying a string on a short stick or dowel, and attach a magnet to the string (you may want to have more than one pole with a large group).

Tape large pieces of newsprint on the wall and have the children stand against them. Use a marker to draw an outline around each player. This is where they will tape what they "catch."

Put all the cards on the floor behind a partition, a table, or screen. Let the children "fish" for the cards with a time limit, or a limit on the number of cards they can get. When they finish their turn, let them tape their cards on their picture. If you let them have crayons, they can also color their picture while waiting for another turn to fish. Fishing for the cards, waiting for a turn or helping younger children are all exercises in patience. Discuss how we can draw positive feelings and experiences to us with patience.

Materials needed: 3x5 cards prepared with words, paper clips, string, dowels, magnets, tape, newsprint, markers, something for a screen

Exploring Patience

Creation Station

Draw the Ocean Depths

Let the children work together on a large piece of paper, or individually on standard size paper, to make ocean pictures.

Separate out all the blue and green crayons or markers before class. Divide the paper into three horiontal sections for surface waves, busy shallow waters and the dark ocean deep.

Remind them that they can move their consciousness into these different levels, with practice.

Materials needed: plain paper, crayons or markers in blue and green color family

Music

Use Music

Deep Voices, produced by Roger Payne
Recordings of humpback, blue and right whales.

Ocean Dreams, by Dean Evenson produced by Soundings of the Planet
Flute, harp and synthesizer music with ocean sounds, dolphins and whales.

Book Shelf

Tell Stories

The King and His Hawk, by James Baldwin in *The Children's Book of Virtues*. Edited by William J. Bennet. The king's impatience brings disastrous results. A powerful story not for the very young.

Horton Hatches an Egg, by Dr. Seuss
Horton goes through all manner of tests and trials but never gives up on his promise to keep the egg warm until it hatches.

The Magic of Patience, a Jataka Tale illus. by Rosalyn White, Dharma Publishing. A mischievous monkey tests the patience of a water buffalo.

Acorn Magic, by Maggie Stern
Simon is a young boy who is so impatient for something to happen that he misses many opportunities to experience what he is looking for. He learns that magical things can happen if you wait and watch carefully.

How Long?, by Eliabeth Dale
A warm sweet story about a little mouse who is learning how to measure time and also learns that some things, like a mother's love, are beyond time or measurement.

Understanding Patience

*P*atience, it has been well said, *is the shortest path to God.* To attune the heart to the rhythms of Eternity, one must first adjust himself to life's longer rhythms. He should not allow his mind to become absorbed in concentration on the little ripples at the surface of the sea.

Patience means also adjusting to whatever is in life, rather than wishing it were something else. Patience is a prerequisite for every type of success. For it is when we work with things as they are that we can change them to whatever we might like them to be.

J. Donald Walters
Affirmations for Self-Healing

 Be not perplexed, Be not afraid, Everything passes, God does not change. Patience wins all things. He who has God lacks nothing; God alone suffices.
St Teresa of Avila

 Patience is never wasted; patience is a process through which a soul passes and becomes precious. Souls who have risen above the world's limitations and sorrows, the world's falseness and deception, they are the souls who have passed through patience.
Harat Inayat Khan

 At the bottom of patience is heaven.
Kanuri (African) Proverb

 Do you have the patience to wait till your mud settles and the water is clear? Can you remain unmoving till the right action arises by itself?
Lao-Tu, Tao-te Ching

I am like the ocean deep, untouched by storm or change.

If you are trying to build a strong relationship, you work on your listening skills, because the ability to listen with an open, loving heart is required for success and growth when relating to others. The most important relationship we ever develop is our relationship with God. When we talk to God, we call it prayer. When we take the time to listen to God with an open, loving heart, we call it meditation.

Spiritual seekers readily accept the idea of daily prayer. Daily meditation is an idea that meets more resistance. Perhaps this is because it is believed that meditation has to be time consuming and complicated to succeed. Begin with the idea that after talking with God, you give equal time to listening. Put that simply, it is possible for even young children to begin to meditate, and to feel the peace of mind that will inevitably come as a result.

········ Fold ········

In inner silence, I feel God's peace.

PRAYER: Dear Lord, Help me to be still and find the peace within that is Thy presence.

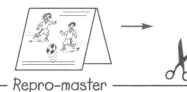

Repro-master

Quiet Fun

Find Your Inner Temple

Use this visualization to help the children imagine going within to their inner temple. Make sure everyone is comfortable, in their own space. Turn the lights down and turn on some soft music to accompany your voice. Read the visualization several times beforehand and use your own words. You will also find tips on meditating with children in this chapter.

Imagine you are taking a walk into a lovely park. As you enter the park and walk down the lane, the noises of the city and the traffic gradually fade. You notice the trees and the flowers and the grass and you stop thinking about all the other things you have to do. (Pause briefly and let the image become clear to everyone.)

You come upon a beautiful quiet spot with a small building that appears to be a temple of some kind. It is so quiet and peaceful here that you don't want to go any farther. There is a neat little path leading up to the door of the temple. The door is shining like gold and it is slightly open. As you walk up to take a closer look, it opens a bit more and you get a glimpse of soft warm light inside. It seems to be welcoming you, so you approach the door and push it open. (At this time you may want to dim the lights further and light a candle.)

As you enter the temple, the door closes softly behind you, but you know you are safe. You can sense the love and acceptance coming from all around you. You have never seen a place so beautiful, but simple. There is velvety blue carpet and the walls seem to glow softly. A single candle is burning, but it doesn't seem to melt. Somehow you know that this is a place to be still and listen. You sit down in front of the candle and feel yourself becoming very calm and quiet inside. Your breathing is slow and quiet, your body is relaxed and still, even your heartbeat seems to be quieter and calmer. The peace you feel within is deep and sweet.

You get up to leave slowly, not feeling rushed at all. You look around and you know this is your temple and you will be back. You walk out into the sunlight and the peace within is still there with you. You say a prayer of thanks for your temple.

Turn the lights up and let everyone stretch and get up. Let them discuss how they felt, or draw pictures of their temple. Explain that meditating is like going into your own inner temple, any time you want to.

Listen Deeply

Explain to the children that you will be using sound as a way to shift your awareness from outside to inside. *Aum* is the sound, or vibration, of all creation and we can tune into that vibration when we turn our attention inward.

Practice saying *Aum* (or *Om*) together. Show the children how to take a deep breath through the nose and say the word with the throat relaxed, chest expanded. After everyone is able to say it strongly together, show them how to cup their hands over their ears and repeat the word together several more times, strongly. Repeat the word several more times in quieter and softer tones until you are all just whispering. Keep your hands over your ears for a few moments while you sit in silence together. If possible, continue the silence a few more moments while everyone puts their hands down.

It can be fun to meditate on other sounds as well, such as a large gong that gives a deep, lasting tone; bell chimes, or notes played on a string instrument such as a cello, bass or harp.

Materials needed: musical instruments optional

Creation Station

Create Alone Pictures

Find a picture without people in a magazine or book that shows different places a person could be alone. Perhaps a scene with a house, yard, tree, river, or hill with a pretty view. Ask the children where they would go in this picture to be alone. Would they like to be out in the open to watch the sunset? Or would they rather be in a treehouse or under a bush, hidden from view?

Let the children draw a picture of their favorite alone place, real or imaginary. You could let them look through magazines for pictures they like and then have them draw themselves in the picture.

Discuss what the children do when they have an opportunity to be alone. Have any of them tried praying or meditating when they are alone?

Materials needed: pictures from magazines, crayons, paper

Tell Stories

Starbright, Meditations for Children, by Maureen Garth
If you need ideas for guiding visualizations or how to make meditation more fun for children, this is a great resource. Always read and reread your selection before using it in class.

Book Shelf

Fly Like a Butterfly, by Shakta Kaur Khalsa
A beginner's book that leads the reader through body movements, yoga postures, stories, songs and quiet meditations. Pictures of young yoga students joyfully doing the activities are on every page. If you have any inhibitions about yoga or meditation with children, this book will resolve them.

Secret Places, Poems selected by Charlotte Huck
Everyone is drawn to a secret place of solitude at some time in their life. These poems from a wide variety of authors describe many such places and can lead to meaningful discussion of the value of solitude and quiet reflection. Where is your secret place?

Days with Frog and Toad, "Alone," by Arnold Lobel
Toad teaches his friend, Frog, that quiet time alone can be special and it doesn't mean you don't like being with your friends. *(Continued)*

Parable of the builders, Matthew 7:24-27

A fun version of this story for young children is in ***Stories Jesus Told*** by Nick Butterworth and Mike Inkpen. Explain to the children that Christ told this story to remind us that with an inner life of prayer and meditation gives us a solid foundation to cope with all the things our outer life demands of us.

Build on Sand

Read the parable about the man who built his house upon sand and then let the children try it. Use a large basin with sand in the bottom and give the children building blocks to build with. After they have built their structure, pour a pitcher of water over the sand and demonstrate how the foundation washes away.

An alternative would be to put some pillows on the floor and let them try building a tower of blocks with a pillow as a foundation. Then let them jump around the pillows and shake their towers down.

If you have time, let everyone build a big tower together on a stable foundation, such as the floor or a sturdy table. Discuss how our *outer life* is like the house the man built and our *inner life* is the foundation that determines if we are strong and unshakable, or weak and uncertain.

Materials needed: large basin, sand, pitcher of water, building blocks, pillows

Use Music

Lord Most High Instrumental piece from *I Came From Joy!* music recording
Rainbows and Waterfalls and ***Krishna's Flute*** produced by Clarity Sound & Light.

Learn Meditation

Some tips on meditation with children:

Atmosphere A special atmosphere for prayer and meditation can help deepen concentration and create a sense of wonder. Preparations can involve simply turning down the lights and gathering everyone in the area of the room that is the least distracting. Or you can arrange one area for devotional activities. An altar helps draw attention away from worldly concerns; however, a vase of flowers, a beautiful picture, or a candle can serve the same purpose. Let the children choose pictures or items for the altar that inspire them. Spread a special blanket on the floor for everyone to sit on, or give each child a bench, cushion or mat to sit on that is used only for meditation. Music is valuable for creating a peaceful atmosphere and for masking outside noises.

Try different approaches, but don't change too many elements at once. Children will find comfort in a routine mind in familiarity with what is expected of them.

Posture and Breath Calm breathing helps to calm the body and mind. A transitional activity such as a story or yoga postures will help bridge active games and quiet time. After the children are sitting instruct them to inhale deeply through their nose, tense their whole body, and then blow out their breath through their mouth, as they relax and let go of the tension. Do this 2-3 times. Another breath-calming activity is to count slowly to five during inhalation, hold the breath while mentally counting to five, and exhale slowly, counting to five again.

If the children are sitting, a straight spine is essential for concentration and alertness. Explain that energy flows up the spine to the spiritual eye (between the eyebrows) and a straight spine enables the energy to flow unobstructed. This also increases our receptivity, like an antenna on a radio. An altar or focal point keeps self-conscious children from staring at one another. When the eyes are closed it is helpful to guide them to visualize a light at the spiritual eye, or to focus on their breath. Explain that concentration at the spiritual eye helps to send their thoughts and prayers to the Divine, as an address on a letter helps the letter get to the right place.

Lying down on the floor is a good option, especially for young children who are wiggly. It may also help them feel less self-conscious about classmates looking at them while they have their eyes closed. You may want to try putting a focal point on the ceiling, such as a picture or glow-in-the-dark stars. Again, a straight spine is important, so flat on the back, with hands at the side is the best pose. To increase awareness of the breath, instruct the children to place their hands on their abdomen and feel it rise and fall as they breathe.

Timing Timing a meditation activity may relieve some anxiety about how long to sit in silence. It may also give you a means to measure the children's progress as they practice periods of stillness. If you find that timing the meditation prevents you from being flexible and flowing with what is happening in the group, however, try doing the activities without a clock for a while.

Start with a prayer. Practice before class and time how long your prayers last. Then tell the children you will be sitting in stillness after the prayer for an equal amount of time. This may only be 15 seconds, but it is a good place to start.

Recognize the children's efforts and let them know they are doing well. Tell them you will gently touch them on the forehead as you walk among them to let them know you notice their calmness. Use a gong or chimes to measure intervals of 10 or 15 seconds and tell the children they should be still and calm until they hear the third chime. When they are ready, you may try playing a piece of music that lasts 2-3 minutes and encourage the children to keep their bodies still through the entire piece. Challenge the children to stretch their meditation time once in a while, and reward success with an extra story or a fresh flower from your altar or another treat.

Understanding Peace of Mind

Peace of mind is the result, not of money in the bank, but of prayer and meditation. The more one contacts God in meditation, the more he feels descending upon him a blanket, as it were, of inner peace, cooling his body, calming his restless impulses, and thrilling his nerves with ever-new delight. Peace is like a weightless waterfall, washing away all worries, and bestowing a new, glad sense of confidence.

Peace of mind is his who knows that God is his only Treasury!

J. Donald Walters
Affirmations for Self-Healing

 Where there is peace and meditation, there is neither anxiety nor doubt.
Saint Francis of Assisi

 Be still, and know that I am God.
Psalm 46:10

 The God of all wants to enter into communion with man. All the age-old history of Christian mysticism, even with some of its most sublime expressions, can speak only imperfectly to us about the unutterable presence of God in our hearts.
Pope John Paul II

In inner silence, I feel God's peace.

*O*ur desire to protect our children is deeply rooted, with good cause. It helps us to fulfill our caretakers' role. In that sincere desire to protect, we can strap on protective padding until our little ones can't move, or we can immobilize them with fearful warnings of life's dangers. But all that worry and fear will kill the joy life holds, for adult and child alike. We must do what we can with the knowledge that when they are not within the safety of our arms, they are held in the arms of their Divine Mother and Father.

Visualize your children surrounded with light and lift them up, mentally, to the Christ center, the point between the eyebrows. Offer them into the Lord's keeping with gratitude and love. Practice this every day and you and your children will learn the security of God's presence together.

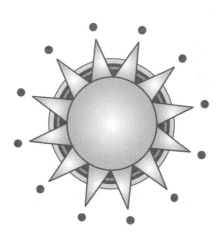

······ Fold ··

I am secure in God's light and love.

PRAYER: I do not worry, because You are always here, Lord.

 — Repro-master —

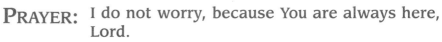

Body Work

Give Me Light!

It is not just marketing that makes all types of glow-in-the-dark toys popular. Light gives us power against darkness, whether real or imagined. Inexpensive flashlights, such as the squeeze kind that come several to a package, can be used in a variety of games.

While the children are out of the room, have a helper scatter small cards around the classroom. Make your own cards with uplifting thoughts or pictures, or purchase small Angel Cards® (see *Appendix*) or tokens. Don't hide the cards *under* things, they have to be visible by flashlight. Let each child have a flashlight and hunt for as many of the cards as they can find in the dark. Count them, read them, share them, and then they will probably want to do it all over again.

An alternative to the game above would be to use plastic glow-in-the-dark stars, made for sticking to the ceiling. Charge the stars under a lamp and scatter them around the room. They would be fun to find without flashlights. They also lose their glow after a short time, which would challenge the children with a time limit.

Materials needed: flashlights for each child, small cards, or plastic glow-in-the-dark stars

Quiet Fun

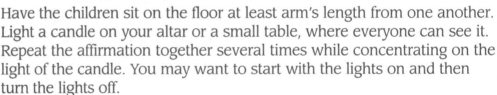

Write it Down

Have the children sit on the floor at least arm's length from one another. Light a candle on your altar or a small table, where everyone can see it. Repeat the affirmation together several times while concentrating on the light of the candle. You may want to start with the lights on and then turn the lights off.

After they know the words well, show them how to "write " the words of the affirmation on the floor with their finger. While sitting in the same spot, turn in a complete circle, writing the words on the floor until you have surrounded yourself with the invisible affirmation. Then blow out the candle and repeat the affirmation several times in the dark.

Encourage them to use the affirmation anytime they are worried. They can use the invisible writing technique on their pillow before going to sleep. Remind them that the Divine Light is shining within them and upon them, even in the dark.

Materials needed: candle

Exploring Security

Creation Station

Draw a Dream

After looking at the affirmation picture with the children, give them blank paper to draw on. Suggest that they draw a balloon to go over the sleeping child's head with pictures of what she is dreaming, or draw a beautiful quilt to go on the bed that would help make her feel safe and happy.

Materials needed: paper, crayons, markers

Music

Use Music

Joy, Joy, Joy from *I Came From Joy!* music recording
A song with both power and sweetness. Good for singing in rounds.

Sing Out with Joy! *I Came From Joy!* music recording

Book Shelf

Tell Stories

Where the Wild Things Are, by Maurice Sendak
Monsters scare Max in his dreams until he learns to face them and take control. Then his nights are fun adventures.

Runaway Bunny, by Margaret Wise Brown
No matter where bunny goes, his mother is always with him, just as our Divine Mother is.

The Always Prayer Shawl, by Sheldon Oberman
Adam's life changes in many ways as he grows up, immigrates to America, marries, raises children and grows old. Through it all though, he is always Adam and he prays with his always prayer shawl that belonged to his grandfather. He teaches his grandson that some things always change and some things never do. Discuss how our relationship with God is the only constant in the universe, and can always be depended upon.

Psalm Twenty-Three, illustrated by Tim Ladwig
The inspirational poem is realistically illustrated and set in a contemporary inner city setting. An African-American boy and his sister have a safe haven in their home filled with love, amidst the dangers and darkness of the city. A relevant and inspirational book for many, but not for the very young.

Understand

Man struggles all his life to store up treasures for himself, to insure his property against loss and his health against the devastation of disease. He rests his faith in outward measures, and sees not that such faith is like asking a wave not to move!

Security is his alone whose faith rests in the Lord. Most practical of men is he who offers his life to God, praying, "My safety is Thy responsibility, Lord." This does not mean we should not be conscientious. But after doing our very best, we should leave the worrying to God!

J. Donald Walters
Affirmations for Self-Healing

And I said to the man who stood at the gate of the year: "Give me a light that I may tread safely in the unknown." And he replied: "Go out into the darkness and put your hand into the hand of God. That shall be to you better than a light, and safer than a known way."
Minnie Louise Haskins

The Lord shall preserve thee from all evil: he shall preserve thy soul. The Lord shall preserve thy going out and thy coming in from this time forth, and even for evermore.
Psalms 121:7-8

No coward soul is mine, No trembler in the world's storm troubled sphere: I see heaven's glories shine, And faith shines equal, arming me from fear.
Emily Bronte

I am secure in God's light and love.

Self-control is really more than learning to sit still and be quiet at the appropriate times. But how to explain this to children? It may be easier to understand if we tell them it is as if there are two selves within each of us. Like two siblings, they each want our attention. Our physical self is the proverbial squeaky wheel that speaks in such a loud, insistent voice that it commands our energy, our choices and our thoughts most of the time. Self-control quiets this self so the small, quiet voice of our inner Self can be heard. Our happiness really depends on whether we listen to our inner Self, or whether we drown it out with material distractions and desires. The physical self is also known as ego; the inner Self may be referred to as the higher Self, the spirit Self, or the true Self.

Children can learn to listen to both selves and meet the needs of both. It takes effort and awareness, but balance and harmony are the result.

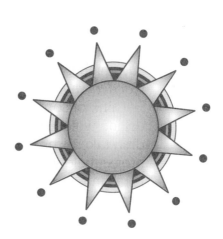

Repro-master

· Fold · ·

All I need is within.

PRAYER: Show me Your sweetness within me, Lord.

Exploring Self-Control

Quiet Fun

Who Said That?

Make two lists, one of things the ego self might say, and one of things the higher Self might say. Examples: *Dinner better be ready soon, or I'll die from hunger.* (ego self) *The prayer time in church is nice, I wish we could do that at home.* (higher Self) *I hope we go to the mall today, maybe Mom will buy me something.* (ego self) *I could listen to the sound of the ocean all day.* (higher Self) *I hate cold weather, I can't wait until summer.* (ego self) *I wonder what it would be like to live inside a rainbow.* (higher Self)

Think of some other examples and read them to the children. Let them decide which self is talking. You could make index cards and let the children take turns reading them and acting them out. If you do the craft project below, have the children hold up their pictures to show which self is talking. Encourage the children to come up with their own ideas. When do you usually hear your higher Self? When is your ego self the loudest voice you hear?

Materials needed: index cards, list of ideas

Body Work

Balancing Act

Make a list of actions appropriate for your age group and setting. Examples: *crawl, skip, take giant steps, tip toe, run in slow motion, inch worm, pirouette, side step*, etc. (Remember many actions can also be done backwards.) Write each action on a piece of the same colored paper, and make an identical set on paper of a different color. Construct a balance scale as explained in the *appendix* of this book. Label each side of the scale with one of your colors.

Each child picks a piece of paper out of a sack, moves to the other side of the room, using the action described, and places a cotton ball on the side of the scale that matches the color of their paper. The child then comes back to you and puts the paper back into the sack with the others. Everyone wins if the scale is balanced after everyone has a turn. You could omit the scale and just use buckets or bags for the cotton balls. Count the number of balls after everyone has a turn. Discuss how we can balance our two selves if we practice self-control with awareness.

A variation of this game would be to give everyone a bunch of cotton balls, and line them up equal distance from the scale (or pair of buckets). Give a short time limit and let everyone throw cotton balls at the scale until time is up. Explain that they are trying to balance the scale by throwing an equal number of balls onto each side of the scale. Everyone wins if they can balance the scale. (Not an easy task!) Discuss how making conscious choices and learning self-control will lead to more balance than if we just act out "hit or miss" and hope it all comes out okay.

Materials needed: cotton balls, colored paper, sack, scale (see appendix)

Exploring Self-Control

Creation Station

Self Signs

To illustrate the idea of two selves within — give each child two paper plates of different colors. Help them decorate the face of one plate with pictures of what their ego self is interested in. Then decorate the face of the other plate with things their higher Self is interested in.

You can provide magazines to cut up to help with ideas. Older children can write words also. Glue the two plates together, with the picture sides facing out. Add a handle to hold onto, using a craft stick or short dowel. Discourage the idea that one side is "good" and the other "bad." Can they think of balanced activities that could belong to both sides? For instance, good food joyfully prepared and shared physical exercise while enjoying nature or buying beautiful things that inspire happy thoughts.

Materials needed: dinner size paper plates in two colors, craft sticks, glue, scissors, markers, crayons, magazines to cut out

Tell Stories

Book Shelf

Monkey Sunday, by Sanna Stanley
A joyful story set in a village in the Congo. A little girl really wants to show her father she can sit still while he preaches, but the animals have other plans for the celebration.

The Stonecutter, by Pam Newton
The hardworking stonecutter is granted his heart's desire, and becomes more than he ever dreamed. After his transformation he realies that the simple happiness he had as a stonecutter was all he could ever wish for.

If You Give a Mouse a Cookie, by Laura Joffe Numeroff
A hilarious tale of a mouse with endless desires, and a boy who tries to fulfill every one, only to find out there is no end. A great opportunity to look at our own endless desires with good-natured humor. A classic, and the best of all the spin-offs that came after this book.

Use Music

Music

Joy, Joy, Joy (sing to the tune *Row, Row, Row Your Boat*)

Joy, Joy, Joy, is ours.
It's always here inside (hands over heart)
It's inside, (hands on chest)
It's outside, (hands out to sides)
It's everywhere, (hands moving all around)
Joy doesn't like to hide. (hands over eyes)

Sing additional verses: *Light, Love, Peace is ours…*

Rise in Freedom and ***Be Free, Inside*** from *I Came From Joy!* music recording.

Understanding Self-Control

Understand

If a lake is made to feed into too many streams, it will soon become drained. Similarly, if a person's heart energies are fed into countless streamlets of desires, he becomes drained, eventually, of even the power to feel. Sated with pleasure, he grows dry, blasé, and indifferent to even the greatest wonders.

The sensualist imagines that by giving up his pleasures he would renounce happiness. But in fact, the more one restrains his senses and learns to live in the peace of the inner Self, the more he finds himself glowing with happiness, good health, and a radiant sense of freedom and well-being.

J. Donald Walters
Affirmations for Self-Healing

Whatever we learn to do, we learn by actually doing it: men come to be builders, for instance, by building, and harp players by playing the harp. In the same way, by doing just acts, we come to be just; by doing self-controlled acts, we come to be self-controlled; and by doing brave acts, we become brave.
Aristotle

Whenever you are to do a thing tho' it can never be known but to your-self, ask yourself how you would act were all the world looking at you, and act accordingly.
Thomas Jefferson
to nephew, Peter Carr

For I do nothing but go about persuading you all, old and young alike, not to take thought for your persons or properties, but first and chiefly to care about the greatest improvements of the soul.
Plato

All I need is within.

Young children seem to delight in finding similarities and connections in the world around them. My child cries, "Look! That car is exactly like ours!" After noting to myself that the car he is pointing to is a different make, model, shape and size than our car; I realize the color is close to the same shade as ours. He is pleased beyond measure when I agree, "Yes, that car is the same color!" I have seen children become immediate friends because their hair is done the same way or their shoes are the same style.

We fine-tune our children's observation skills to see differences, instead of similarities. "One of these things is not like the others" and "Find ten differences between these two pictures," are games most children play countless times before they reach school. We can relearn how to see the sameness in the world from our children. We, in turn, can help them to see and feel a connection to the universe that goes beyond color, size, and shape by teaching them that we are a part of all that is in a very real sense. God did not just create the universe, God became the universe, and all creation has the same divine origin.

Repro-master

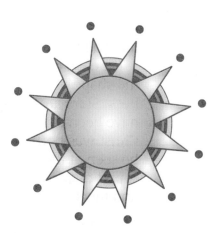

---- Fold --

I feel a part of all God's creation.

PRAYER: Beloved Spirit, help me feel Your presence within myself and all that is.

Exploring Self-Expansion

Body Work

Discover We Are All Stars

Use colored yarn to make the shape of a five pointed star on the wall. If there is enough space, make several stars in different sizes, ranging from about 3 ft. tall to 5 ft. tall. Anchor each point and angle to the wall with tape. You can do the same thing on the floor with tape if you don't have the wall space. Chalk on the sidewalk outside is another option.

Let each child stand against the wall with arms spread out, to fit into the shape of the star. Talk about how stars twinkle and shine in the darkness. Stars are used by sailors to find direction while out at sea. Stars have been used as symbols of goodness and light since time began. Christ was born under a special star. We all have an inner star that can be seen at the spiritual eye during deep meditation. Who made the stars? A part of God became the stars and a part of God became you, so you and the stars are the same!

Materials needed: colored yarn, tape

Creation Station

Build a Poem

Remember the old nursery rhyme *The House that Jack Built*? That poem was done in the cumulative style, which tells the story of how things are connected in an amusing way. Your class can write their own poem, building on the line... *in the universe that God created*.

Older children could tackle this on their own, but even very young children can participate in a group effort. Use a white board and build the poem line by line. The structure usually starts with something small and grows to the final line (*this is the bird that lives in the tree that shades the meadow that feeds the horses....in the universe that God created*). If it seems easier to work backwards, you can change it when you write it out later.

This will challenge the children to think of each item in the poem, and explain how it could be related to the next. They will probably come up with many possibilities. Let everyone contribute; the poem can be as long as you want. Write it out for them and let them illustrate it. You may also find ways to act it out or tell it with a puppet show.

Materials needed: white board and pens

Exploring Self-Expansion

Play "Go Togethers"

Fill a box or bag with an assortment of small items. Check your garage or basement for various bits of hardware and what-nots. The bigger the assortment, the more fun this will be.

Put the items on the table or floor and challenge the children to sort them and put them into groups, using their own criteria for sameness. See if they come up with groups by function (things from the kitchen), or size (things smaller than my hand), or material (everything plastic), or texture (things that are soft), or other categories you didn't even consider. Large groups can be split into teams. The same items can be sorted many times with different results.

Discuss how it is possible to see connections between people or things that others may not see. Explain how we can practice and work on expanding our vision to include all of creation in our reality, until everything and everyone is connected to us in some way.

Materials needed: large assortment of household items

Tell Stories

Grass Sandals, the Travels of Basho, by Dawnine Spivak
A beautifully told story of Basho, one of the best-loved poets of Japan. The simplicity of his life and the connection he had with all creation is expressed in the haiku poetry and the beautiful illustrations by Demi.

The Tree in the Ancient Forest, by Carol Reed-Jones
This cumulative poem illustrates the interdependence of plant and animal life, with lush illustrations that bring the forest up close.

One Night, A Story from the Desert, by Cristina Kessler
The harsh Sahara desert is where Muhamed, a young Tuareg boy, is most at home. He feels that he is "the wealthiest of boys", with his loving family and animal friends. A night alone in the desert is a great blessing for him, and not the frightening experience we would think it to be.

Use Music

Channels
Woodland Devas
Hello There, Brother Bluebell
from *I Came From Joy!* music recording

Understanding Self-Expansion

Understand

Self-expansion is the essence of all aspiration. Why do we seek to possess all things? Because by acquisition we imagine we'll expand our dominion. Why do we seek to learn more? Because we think by enlarging our knowledge we expand our understanding. And why do we seek ever-new experiences? Because we believe that, through them, we'll expand our awareness. When you stretch a lump of dough outward, it becomes not only broader, but thinner. Such often is the case when we stretch the mind only outwardly. Reaching out too far, we sacrifice depth in our lives.

The Self-expansion toward which all life aspires is of the spirit: an expansion of sympathy, of love, of the awareness that comes from sensing God's presence everywhere.

J. Donald Walters
Affirmations for Self-Healing

That I am part of the earth my feet know perfectly, and my blood is part of the sea.
D.H. Lawrence

Whither shall I go from thy Spirit? Or whither shall I flee from thy presence?
Psalms 139:7

Thou art a second world in miniature, the sun and moon are within thee, and also the stars.
Origen

I feel a part of all God's creation.

*Y*oung children are usually eager to be helpers. They are anxious to learn new skills and show us their independence. The genuine pleasure a young child feels when she is able to help someone expands her sense of self and strengthens her connections to others. As children grow, they become more absorbed in their own needs and the idea of spontaneously serving others may grow dim. But we can help our children keep that "Let me help!" attitude by teaching them how service can be an expression of their true Self, unique and important.

We are surrounded by examples of service. Acts of service that gain the most attention however, are usually dramatic acts of heroism full of danger and personal sacrifice. It is important for us to understand, and teach our children, that we need not wait for a crisis or global emergency to serve others. If we pay attention, opportunities to serve others are constant and varied, in every part of our daily lives. Recognizing acts of service and being grateful to those individuals, is the first step in expanding the spirit. Being serviceful allows us to deepen our connection with the Spirit Within All.

Repro-master

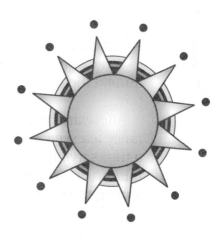

Fold

I serve
God
through
others.

PRAYER: Divine Mother, show me new ways to serve Thee by helping those around me.

Exploring Service

Body Work

Learn About Service

Play games to explore all the meanings of the word *service*. This word has many uses and can conjure up many images. Badminton rackets can be used to serve shuttlecocks over a net of chairs. Trays can be used to carry paper cups that are *served* to another player. Give each player a toy car and let them take it through a pretend *service* station.

You can make each activity into a relay game. Or set up stations around the room and rotate the children to each station for a period of time.

Afterwards, sit down together and *serve* a snack, or *serve* juice in a fancy tea *service*. Bring a variety of small snacks and let each child have a turn serving something to the others. Ask everyone how it feels to be the server. Discuss all the ways we use the word *service*. Why do we call joining the military going into the *service*? Why is a Sunday morning church ritual called a *service*?

Materials needed: serving trays, badminton rackets and shuttle-cocks, toy cars, tea service, paper cups

Find 5 Ways to Serve

Quiet Fun

Help your children to reach beyond the idea that serving is limited to performing a physical task for someone and understand the many ways to be of service to others. Five possible categories of service could be: 1) good deeds, 2) sharing possessions, 3) good thoughts, 4) praying for others, 5) meditation, or growing spiritually. Performing a task that helps others and sharing possessions are easy to see as serviceful. Most children will eagerly participate in praying for others, especially those close to them. Simply having good thoughts can help others by bringing more light into the world. A cheerful smile, a loving blessing, an attitude of service can help others in a very real way.

The idea of serving others by meditating or growing spiritually may be more difficult for children to understand. This is really an extension of having good thoughts. By growing in our spiritual life, through meditation or other spiritual practices, we become better at serving in every way. We learn to see opportunities for service and we respond to the opportunities with willingness and love.

Read a story recommended here, or one of your own choosing. Ask the children to identify what kind of service they see performed in the story. Are there opportunities for service that the characters did not act upon? How would the story be different if the characters were more serviceful? Can the story be changed to include all five types of service? Can the children think of other familiar tales that show examples of service?

Exploring Service

Creation Station

Give each child a piece of paper big enough to place both hands on, side by side. Help them to trace around each hand with a marker. Label the fingers of one hand with the five types of service discussed in the last activity. Label the fingers of the other hand with the five words of the affirmation. Let each child decorate their picture.

Older children can cut out the hands and glue them on another colored sheet of paper. Cut out all the hands and decorate a bulletin board. Photocopy one of the pictures to use as an invitation or announcement of a class service project. The pictures can also be used as a thank you note for someone who has helped the class through an act of service.

Materials needed: paper, markers, crayons, scissors

Music

Use Music

Many Hands Make a Miracle, from *I Came From Joy!* music recording

A fun, energetic song about service. Make up motions to accompany the words.

Book Shelf

Tell Stories

Miss Tizzy, by Libba Moore Gray
Miss Tizzy is the most peculiar and most beloved old lady in the neighborhood. She gives of herself without thought of return. But when she is in need, the children show her that they have learned her lessons very well.

Captain Jonathan Sails the Sea, by Wolfgang Slawski
Captain Jonathan treats his tugboat crew to a trip of a lifetime to exotic, faraway places. They have wonderful adventures, but Captain Jonathan finds his happiness lies in just being useful back in his own harbor.

People Who Helped the World, a series by Gareth Stevens Publishing
This series of biographies is for advanced young readers. But they provide a great deal of information and pictures with an emphasis on what influenced these great souls, and how they made a difference to the world. Included in the series are Marie Curie, Father Damien, Mahatma Gandhi, Bob Geldof, and Martin Luther King, Jr.

Understanding Service

Understand

Service is ennobling. It is a way of offering our human littleness into the great Reality that is God. Service should not be given with the thought that one is serving people, merely. It should be given with an inward consciousness to the Lord Who resides in all creatures. When we serve others in this spirit, we find our own spirits becoming freed from egotism. Peace then fills us, in the realization that there isn't anyone with whom we need compete.

What joy, to think that we belong to God!

J. Donald Walters
Affirmations for Self-Healing

 The state of freedom from action (that is, of eternal rest in the Spirit) cannot be achieved without action. No one, by mere renunciation and outward non-involvement, can attain perfection.
Bhagavad Gita 3:4

 "God is helping God," Master replied with a sweet smile. "That is the nature of His cosmic drama."
Paramhansa Yogananda

 Thus one should use whatever capacities of body, speech, and mind one has for the benefits of others: That is right.
The Dalai Lama

 A good deed is the best prayer.
Mexican proverb

I serve God through others.

The ability to understand and empathize with another person's reality is a natural developmental step. All young children have to grow to the point of wanting to share with others. At the age of two, whacking other children with their toys is more normal than spontaneously sharing. Forcing children to share all their prized possessions may create resentment and greater determination to gain control and hang on tight to everything.

The truth is, many adults never learn that sharing is more than letting others play with your toys. Sharing is not a way to force our egos to let go of attachments, or prevent our children from forming them. Sharing what we have is a way of expressing our gratitude to God. Real sharing comes when we understand that God is the Infinite Source, and what is given belongs only to God. With that understanding, it becomes simple. We take special care of all we possess, because it's on loan from God. When we are given the opportunity to share what we have, we can do so with a willingness that will insure we will always have what we need.

Repro-master

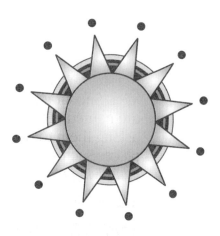

· · · Fold · · ·

When I share what God has given me, happiness grows.

PRAYER: Beloved Friend, teach me the joy of sharing all You share with me.

Exploring Sharing

Learn the ABCs

Make a set of alphabet flashcards before class, or use a small white-board. Sit in a circle with the children and explain that you will be holding up a flashcard, or writing a letter on the board. They must try to name all the things they can think of that can be shared, that begin with that letter.

You can have each child speak in turn, or let them call out their ideas freestyle. You may want to have each child stand up when they have an idea. Encourage discussion about how one could share the things that are named. If the children are non-readers, you can modify this idea by asking them to name things to share that could be found in a particular place. Such as: *What could you share at the park? What could you share in your living room? What could you share on the bus?*

Materials needed: alphabet cards or white board with marker

Play "I share, You share"

Explain to the children that they need to pretend that they own every-thing in the room. A friend has asked for help, because she is starting her own school and needs many things. (If you are in a different setting, change the setting in the story.) Everyone will have a chance to choose something in the room to "share" with this friend.

You start the game by crossing the room and touching something you choose to share. The next player then goes to touch what you touched, and then touches what she wants to share. Each player touches all the previous players' things, and then adds their item. The game gets more difficult as you go, so you may want to let younger players have turns first.

Discuss how sharing helps us remember that all we have comes from God, and that when we share, we are more open to that Infinite Source.

Make a Collage

Using a variety of magazine pictures, greeting cards, old calendars, and other pictures, help the children create a collage of things they can share, or that have been shared with them at one time.

Be sure to have more than just pictures of personal possessions. Encourage other ideas, such as sharing time with someone, sharing a shady spot under a tree, sharing a beautiful view, or sharing a happy thought. Cut out the pictures and glue on heavy paper or cardboard, or combine all the pictures on a bulletin board with the affirmation.

Materials needed: magazines, greeting cards, calendars to cut, scissors, glue, blank paper

Exploring Sharing

Draw Treasure Pictures

Let the children color the affirmation picture and then draw what they think may be in the treasure chest.

Materials needed: crayons, markers, plain paper

Share a Happy Thought

Share a happy experience with the children during the week, between classes. Copy the affirmation picture on a photocopier, and shrink it to fit four images on one page. This will make four images approximately 4x5. Print these on card stock and cut apart, or cut the images and glue to cardboard to make postcards. Send each child a postcard with a happy thought from you.

Materials needed: photocopier, lightweight cardboard, glue, scissors

Use Music

Many Hands Make a Miracle, All the World Is My Friend,
I Came From Joy! music recording

Tell Stories

The Brother's Promise, by Frances Harber
This Jewish folktale tells us "the angels weep with joy" when we share.

The Sign Painter's Dream, by Roger Roth
Clarence is not interested in making a sign for free, but something changes his mind, and changes him.

Nicolas, Where Have You Been? by Leo Lionni
A young mouse learns about sharing from the birds he thought were his enemies.

Pages of Music, by Tony Johnston
Shepherds share their simple life with an artist and her young son. The boy later becomes a famous composer and conductor and shares his music with the shepherds.

Raising Yoder's Barn, by Jane Yolen
A devastating fire destroys an Amish family's barn. The fire and the raising of the new barn are seen through the eyes of Matthew, an eight-year-old Amish boy.

Understand

True happiness is found not in possessions, but in sharing what one has with others. Thus is one's self-identity expanded, as he learns to live in, and enjoy, a greater reality.

People who gladly share with others feel themselves bathed by a constant, inner stream of happiness.

Sharing is the doorway through which the soul escapes the prison of self-preoccupation. It is one of the clearest paths to God.

J. Donald Walters
Affirmations for Self-Healing

God loves a cheerful giver. He gives most who gives with joy.
Mother Teresa of Calcutta

And there are those who give and know not pain in giving, nor do they seek joy, nor give with mindfulness of virtue; they give as in yonder valley the myrtle breathes its fragrance into space. Through the hands of such as these God speaks, and from behind their eyes He smiles upon the earth.
Kahlil Gibran

When I share what God has given me, happiness grows.

*C*hildren face the early challenges of mobility and communication unconcerned with success or failure. Their loved ones encourage every effort, even when the effort results in "failure" or no outward, measurable progress. After those early years, however, children learn quickly how the world measures success in other endeavors. We cannot, and should not, completely shield children from worldly rewards or obstacles, but we can teach and model an alternate measurement. If they learn early to measure their successes by looking *inward*, all of life's challenges can be met with ever increasing awareness and joy.

Every decision we make, every action we take, every attitude we take on, moves us closer to God or farther away. True success can be measured by asking: "Which way am I going?"

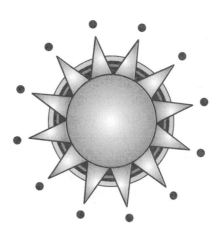

········ Fold ··

What I do today can create a better tomorrow.

PRAYER: Lord, help me move closer to You each time I try something new.

— Repro-master —

Body Work

Play "Move Inward"

Place a heavy chair or sturdy table in the middle of the room. Tie a 4 to 6 ft. length of heavy string or yarn to the chair for each child participating. The children should take up the end of their string and stand equal distances away from the chair, like spokes on a wheel. At the signal, the children must wind the string around one finger, keeping the opposite hand behind their back, and race toward the middle. This is more difficult than it seems, so you will want to vary the length of the string according to the children's ages and abilities. Instruct them to loosen the string as soon as they reach the goal, to prevent a numb finger.

Discuss how we are all connected to a Divine Reality on an inner level, and a connection that cannot be cut or broken. But we can "move away" from this divine center even faster than we can move towards it. Although that divine connection is always there, our actions and attitudes can make it appear very close or very far away. You could let one child sit in the center and help pull others in, acting as a spiritual guide or teacher.

Materials needed: heavy string or yarn, sturdy table or chair

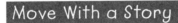

Move With a Story

Quiet Fun

Have the children sit in a circle and place yourself in the center. Read or tell a story that has interesting action by hero and villain, such as *The Stone Lion*.

Explain to the children that our behaviors move us closer or further away from God, or the center of the circle. As you tell the story, ask the children if the character is behaving in a way that moves him closer to God or further away. If the answer is further away, the children move away from the center of the circle. If the answer is closer, then they move into the circle, closer to you. In this way, the children move back and forth, according to the characters' actions, as you tell the story. With older children, you can introduce the idea that the "center" is really not outside us, but within.

Materials needed: a story

Measuring Up

Show the children how we measure with a bathroom scale, a kitchen scale, a ruler, a yardstick, a tape measure, measuring cups and spoons, clothing and shoe sizes, a scale on a map, a clock, a sun dial, a kitchen timer, a thermometer, etc. Let the children try out the tools and measure things in the room.

If you look around, there is evidence of measuring everywhere. We want to know *how much, how far, how long, how big, how small*? It is natural to want to know how we measure up too. Discuss the fact that others will judge, but we must look within to decide if we are moving in the direction we want to go.

Materials needed: measuring tools

Music

Use Music

Move All You Mountains, Sing in the Meadows, Rise in Freedom
I Came From Joy! music recording

Creation Station

Picture Success

What could you do today that would make tomorrow even better? Discuss this question and let the children express different ideas. Ask the children to draw pictures of their ideas.

Materials needed: plain paper, crayons, markers

Book Shelf

Tell Stories

Nim and the War Effort, by Milly Lee
Nim lives with her family in China Town, San Francisco. During WWII, Nim and the other children in her school help the war effort with many projects. The latest is a newspaper drive, and it's a race to see who collects the most newspapers.

Knots on a Counting Rope, by Bill Martin
A young Native American boy is thrilled with doing his best and demonstrates that success isn't always winning.

The Stone Lion, by Alan Schroeder
A cruel older brother learns about true success and humility from his younger brother.

The Principal's New Clothes, by Stephanie Calmenson
This is a very funny and kindly new version of Hans Christian Anderson's fairy tale. We all know the punch line, but this version offers a warm happy feeling to balance the embarrassing predicament the principal puts himself in. Do you think the principal feels more successful in his fancy clothes, or wearing all his friend's clothes at the end of the story?

Understand

True success means transcendence. It means finding what we really want, which is not outward things, but inner peace of mind, self-understanding—and above all, the joy of God.

Outward success means transcendence also. It means rising above past accomplishments to reach new levels of achievement. Success can mean accepting failure, too, when such acceptance helps us to transcend a false ambition. Every failure, moreover, can be a stepping stone to highest achievement.

Success should not be measured by the things accomplished, but by our increasing understanding, ability, and closeness to God.

J. Donald Walters
Affirmations for Self-Healing

Everyone should know that you can't live in any other way than by cultivating the soul.
Thomas Moore

Follow your bliss.
Joseph Campbell

Success is relative. It is what we can make of the mess we have made of things.
T. S. Eliot

The creative spontaneous soul sends forth its promptings of desire and aspiration in us. These promptings are our true fate, which is our business to fulfill. A fate dictated from outside, from theory or from circumstances, is a false fate.
D. H. Lawrence

What I do today can create a better tomorrow.

I have never heard a parent or teacher complain about a child's lack of will power! Strong will is often viewed negatively, however. We must recognize that great will power is required for great achievement and spiritual progress. It must be channeled in the right way, and focused on right action. It must also be attuned to Divine Will or it may be destructive.

Attuning to Divine Will is like plugging into a power source that will never run dry. Our will power is strengthened, which then enables us to tap into an ever stronger flow of divine energy.

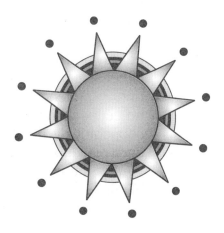

·········· Fold

My will
is to do
that
which
is right
to do.

PRAYER: Divine Friend, guide my will with Thine.

Repro-master

Exploring Will Power

Body Work

Play "Disappearing Obstacles"

Set up an obstacle course that the children have to maneuver through. You can create a fun course with just a few props, such as chairs, pillows, tables. After they have played a bit, explain that an adult volunteer will leave the room briefly, and be blindfolded.

While the volunteer is out of the room, let the children help you quickly and quietly remove the obstacles. Instruct the children to sit on either side of the room and give verbal guidance to the blindfolded volunteer, pretending to guide him around the obstacles. Then let the volunteer back in the room. Some small groups may be able to do this cooperatively, freestyle; or you may want the children to take turns, with each player giving one instruction, such as "take two steps to the left."

After the volunteer reaches the goal across the room, remove the blindfold and reveal that the obstacles were not really there! Discuss how God can minimize or remove apparent obstacles when we attune our will to the Divine Will and we are doing the right thing.

Materials needed: blindfold

Ride in a Horse race

In this horse race, everyone can pretend to be the horse, or the rider. Mark a starting line on the floor, and a finish line on the floor across the room. Divide your class into three groups and assign one of three colors to each group. Or let the children choose one of three colors for themselves.

Crumple up three sheets of paper of each color and place the paper balls in a bag. Explain to the children that they will take turns reaching in the bag and taking out one paper ball, without looking. The color chosen will indicate which "horses" get to move one giant step toward the finish line. If a yellow paper is pulled out of the sack, then the yellow players take one giant step forward. Put the paper ball back in the sack and let another player choose. Continue until one group of horses reach the finish line.

You can add props if you wish. Each player could have a yarn bracelet to indicate their color. Or tape a colored paper, with a number, on their shirt. A spinner or game tokens could be used instead of the paper balls to indicate who moves. Keeping the colors to only three prevents any one player from being singled out as winner or loser. Discuss how our will and Divine Grace, work together to achieve great things—as the horse and rider work together to win the race.

Materials needed: colored paper, paper sack

Have a Seat!

Demonstrate "will power sitting" to the children. Assume a squatting position, back against the wall, thighs parallel to the floor, with no chair. Try it before class and time how long you can maintain this posture. It is difficult, no matter your athletic ability. Challenge the children to try and time their efforts. Explain that this feat requires will power and is not a test of strength or athletic ability. Encourage the children to support everyone's efforts and cheer each other on. Use an assistant to help you time everyone if you have a large group.

Materials needed: stopwatch or watch with second hand

Creation Station

Create a View!

After looking at the affirmation picture, ask the children to draw pictures of what the mountain climber in the picture might see when he gets to the top of the mountain.

Materials needed: paper, crayons, markers

Music

Use Music

Move All You Mountains *I Came From Joy!* music recording

This is a terrific song to do with motions. Just listen to the words and add movements that express the strong will power and energy of the music.

Book Shelf

Tell Stories

Brave Irene, by William Steig
Irene's mother made the duchess a dress for the ball, but she is too sick to deliver it. Irene makes the delivery for her, through a terrible snowstorm and raging wind. She never gives up and never loses sight of her purpose, despite the incredible odds. Irene would inspire any boy or girl.

Horton Hatches an Egg, by Dr. Seuss
Horton goes through all manner of tests and trials but never gives up on his promise to keep the egg warm until it hatches.

Miss Rumphius, by Barbara Cooney
Will power is not only about overcoming big obstacles. Miss Rumphius is inspired to use her will power to achieve the simple goal of adding more beauty to the world. She spreads lupine seeds wherever she goes.

Understanding Will Power

Understand

Will power, and not the vague abstraction luck, is the secret of true achievement. Will power, on subtle energy levels, generates what only looks like luck, by magnetically attracting to us opportunities. Our will is strengthened by removing from our minds the "no-saying" tendency: the obstructions of doubt, of laziness, and of fear—yes, even of the fear of success!

Will power is developed by persevering to the conclusion of whatever one attempts. One should start first with little undertakings, then proceed to bigger ones. Infinite will power comes from harnessing the little human will to God's infinite, all powerful consciousness.

J. Donald Walters
Affirmations for Self-Healing

 Will is to grace, as the horse is to the rider.
Saint Augustine

 There is nothing uncertain about God's will, nor is it something to be feared. It is wise and practical for any person, faced with a crisis or need, to let go of tension and fear by praying, "Father, let Thy will be done in and through me."
Eric Butterworth

 Resolve to perform what you ought; perform without fail what you resolve.
Benjamin Franklin

 A firm resolve pierces even rock.
Japanese proverb

My will is to do that which is right to do.

I have been told that in some alternative schools all activity is called *work*. This probably helps reinforce the ideas that all activities can be enjoyable, and children's activities are important, just as work is for adults. Perhaps because the word, *work*, has thousands of years of hard labor attached to it, I much prefer the idea that everything we do is an opportunity to *play* with our Divine Companion.

Much as children separate *play* (fun), and *work* (not fun), we tend to separate spiritual and non-spiritual activities. It is only our attitude that separates them; it is all the same to God. What we really hope for our children is that they experience an awareness of Spirit in all activities. And when they choose employment, we hope they choose with the thought of service, creativity and inspiration, in addition to interest, skill and income. But what really matters is the attitude, not the chosen profession.

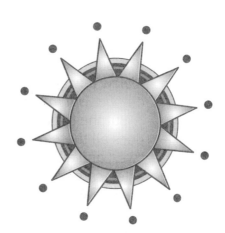

- - - Fold - -

I think of God when I work and play.

Repro-master

PRAYER: Infinite Spirit, thank you for the chance to work and play with You.

Play "We did!"

You can play this simple game anywhere, in the classroom, around the dinner table, or in the car. Each person takes a turn telling the others what they did so far that day. There are no rules about what you have to tell, but it is more fun with some details.

For example: *"After I got up, I had to make my bed. Then I ate a bagel with strawberry jam for breakfast. I got dressed, and put on shorts, because I knew it would be hot. Then I had to clean my room before I could play outside with my friend."*

But the trick is telling everything with plural pronouns because, God does all these things with all of us, every day. Substitute all the "I's" with "we," and all the "my's" with "our," and so on. Everyone else will have to listen carefully and catch the mistakes. Each mistake means a point, and the one with the fewest points at the end wins.

It can be fun to make a list of all the activities mentioned and review them together. Encourage the children to make a habit of reviewing what they did with God every evening, and planning what they will do with their Divine Companion the next day.

Play "And God went too!"

Sit together and start a clapping rhythm by slapping your thighs with open palms, alternated with a clap. Start the game by saying, "I went to the zoo to see the elephants, and God went too!" Keep the words in rhythm with your claps. Each child gets a turn to add an animal to the list and say it again. (...to see the elephants, and the lions, and the tigers, etc.) If anyone forgets to say "...and God went too!," you have to start over.

Color Work Pictures

Give the affirmation picture to the children to color. Point out to them that we can't see the child's face in the picture, so we don't know how he feels about painting the fence. Ask them to put God in the picture with the child. God is always happy when we invite Him to join us, so God would be smiling, even if it is hard work.

OR

Ask the children to draw a picture of the kind of work they would like to do with God when they grow up.

Materials needed: crayons, markers, plain paper

Exploring Work

Body Work

Paint a Rainbow

If you don't have a fence to paint, you can always paint a rainbow. Tell the children that their job is to paint the room with a rainbow of colors. Use a large tub or box as your bucket of "paint." Let each child take a turn getting in the tub and pretending to cover themselves in paint. They also get to choose what color the paint is, of course.

Play some light dancing music to accompany the game. When they get out of the paint tub, encourage them to dance around the room and imagine they are painting everything in beautiful colors of the rainbow. Scarves are fun to use as "paint brushes," if you have them.

When everyone is tired, let them rest on the floor. Turn down the lights a bit and encourage everyone to imagine the room glowing with the beautiful colors they have painted. Say the affirmation together several times and end with a few moments of silence.

Materials needed: large tub, box, or bucket, music, scarves optional

Music

Use Music

Many Hands Make a Miracle *I Came From Joy!* music recording

Blue Danube Waltz, by J. Strauss, and *Sleeping Beauty Waltz*, by Tchaikovsky are fun to dance to.

Book Shelf

Tell Stories

The Giant Carrot, by Jan Peck
This family works together, each by his or her nature, to grow a giant carrot that is harvested with joy. A delightful retelling of a classic folktale.

Seven Loaves of Bread, by Ferida Wolff
When Milly is sick, her sister Rose must bake the bread, but Rose doesn't like to work any more than she has to. Trying NOT to work causes Rose more trouble than she ever imagined.

Grandpa's Garden, by Darian Shea
The granddaughter looks forward to working with Grandpa on Saturdays in his garden. Lessons of growth and change, life and death, as well as pleasure in work come naturally in the garden.

Parable of the Two Sons, Matthew 21:28-32.
Two sons have different attitudes about helping their father. One source for the retelling of the story is *Stories Jesus Told*, by Nick Butterworth and Mick Inkpen.

Understanding Work

Understand

Work should be done with a creative attitude—never for the sake of selfish gain, but for the chance it gives us to help create a better world. Those who work with the thought of pay live in the future; they lose the habit of living here and now, where alone true happiness can be found.

Work should always be done as well as possible—not out of self conceit, but in gratitude for the free gift of life, of sunshine, of water, of air—and in gratitude, simply, for our God-given power to be useful to our fellowman.

> J. Donald Walters
> *Affirmations for Self-Healing*

One must not always think so much about what one should do, but rather what one should be. Our works do not ennoble us; but we must ennoble our works.
> *Meister Eckhart*

To pray is to work, to work is to pray.
> *Benedictine Order Motto*

It is wonderful how much may be done, if we are always doing.
And that you may be always doing good, my dear,
is the ardent prayer of yours affectionately.
> *Thomas Jefferson*
> *to daughter, Martha Jefferson*

I think of God when
I work and play.

Appendix

Introspection

Sweet Butterflies / fig. 1—refer to page 77

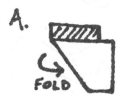

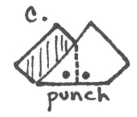

Kindness

Paper People / fig. 2-7—refer to page 82

fig. 2

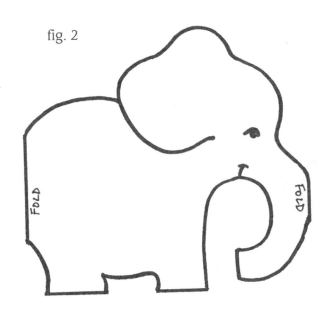

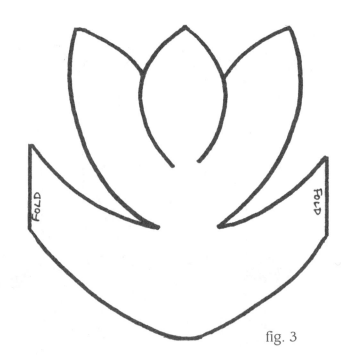

fig. 3

fig. 4

fig. 5

fig. 6

fig. 7

Love
Hugs / fig. 8—refer to page 88

Openness
Radio G-O-D / fig. 9—refer to page 100

Security
—refer to page 120
Angel Cards®, 1981, Drake and Tyler.
Produced by Narada Media. Distributed by
Music Design Inc. Box of small cards with
positive, uplifting words and angel illustrations.

fig. 9

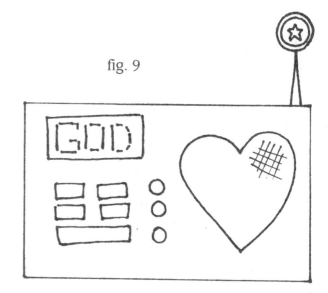

Self Control
Balancing Act / fig. 10—refer to page 126

Fig. 10

Biographical Index

Aesop (?620 - 560 BC): Reputed Greek author of Aesop's Fables.

Aristotle (384 - 322 B.C.): Greek philosopher. Studied with the philosopher Plato, and taught Alexander the Great.

Bhagavad Gita: Hindu sacred text dating from around 500 BC. The Gita is a poem taken from a larger text, the Mahabharata.

Bronte, Emily (1818 - 1848): English novelist, one of three author sisters.

Buddha, Gautama (563 - 483 B.C.): Founder of the Buddhist religion and philosophy. Born into Indian royal family. Buddha is a title meaning "the awakened one."

Butterworth, Eric: Contemporary author, Unity minister, and considered a leading spokesperson on "practical mysticism."

Campbell, Joseph (1904 - 1987): American theorist, writer and lecturer.

Catherine of Genoa (1447 -1510): Italian mystic admired for her work among the poor.

Chesterton, G. K. (1874 - 1936): British writer.

Confucius (551 - 479 B.C.): Chinese sage who founded Confucianism.

D.H., Lawrence (1885 - 1930): English novelist, poet and playwright.

Dalai Lama (1935 -): Spiritual and political leader of Tibetan Buddhists. The title means "the ocean of wisdom." Since the Chinese takeover of Tibet in 1959, the Dalai Lama has lived in exile in India.

DuBois, W.E.B. : Contemporary writer, scholar, activist, and founder of the NAACP.

Eckhart, Meister (1260? - 1327): German Dominican theologian, mystic, and preacher; founder of German mysticism.

Eliot, T. S. (1888 - 1965): U.S. born British poet and dramatist. Awarded Nobel prize in literature 1948.

Emerson, Ralph Waldo (1803 -1882): American poet and Trancendentalist.

Francis of Assisi (1181 - 1226): Beloved Italian saint and mystic. Founder of the Franciscan order.

Resources for Parents and Teachers

Catalogs

Chinaberry, Books and Other Treasures for the Entire Family.
This is a catalog that is more than a catalog. It offers a rich variety of books, gifts and toys for children and parents with in-depth reviews of every item. All the items support and encourage conscious parenting, joyful living and respect for all life. Spiritual themes and stories from many cultures and religions are here with many "just-for-fun" offerings also.
Chinaberry Book Service
2780 Via Orange Way, Suite B
Spring Valley, CA 91978
800-776-2242

The Global Classroom
A catalog of resources for teachers and parents who believe in character and value education. This catalog keeps expanding and offers many practical tools for teaching universal values, conflict resolution, integrating community and family, service learning, cooperative learning, and understanding world religions, cultures, and traditions.
The Global Classroom
12 Winter Sport Lane
Williston, VT 05495
www.globalclassroom.com

The Wellspring Guide, Books for Our Children, Our Families, Our Future
This catalog offers in-depth reviews of books for children and books for adults caring for, parenting and teaching children. The emphasis is on books that support healthy attachment, physical closeness, joyful mothering, and creative toys and play.
The Wellspring Guide
Wellness Associates, 123 Wildwood Trail
Afton, VA 22920
www.TheWellspring.com

Dawn Publications

This company publishes the most beautiful books for reading, sharing, and teaching children. Each one of Dawn's books has a different way of reminding us to love and respect all life, and to care for our earth home. They also offer a series of teacher's guides to accompany some of their picture books.

Dawn Publications
P.O. Box 2010
Nevada City, CA 95959
800-545-7475
www.dawnpub.com

Books

The Joyful Child: A Sourcebook of Activities and Ideas for Releasing Children's Natural Joy
by Peggy Jenkins
This book and others by this author are valuable resources for working joyfully with children. Even if you don't teach in a formal setting, if there are children in your life you will find her suggestions inspiring.

Curriculum of Love: Cultivating the Spiritual Nature of Children
by Morgan Simone Daleo
This book offers a collection of activities for young children, centered on ten core values. The author comes from a background in the performing and creative arts and this is evident in her creative approach to movement, music and hands-on activities.

Supporting the Inner Life of Your Child
by Toby Moorhouse
A small book with a lot to offer about helping children explore their spiritual identity.
Education for Life Foundation
14618 Tyler Foote Road
Nevada City, CA 95959

Sharing Nature with Children and Sharing Nature with Children II
by Joseph Cornell
These two books have won international acclaim as practical, useable guides for exploring the world of nature. Used by families, schools, youth groups, scouts, city dwellers and naturalists of all ages.

Valerie and Walter's Best Books for Children
by Valerie V. Lewis
and Walter M. Mayes
An enthusiastic guide for choosing children's books for all ages and reading levels. Thoughtful and practical, with many cross-references by theme and interest. Hints and valuable advice are written in a friendly conversational tone. If you are searching for children's books for any reason, you will want one of these.

Sources for Quotations

Breakfast with the Pope: Daily Readings
Pope John Paul II
Selected by the editors of Servant Publications 1995
Servant Publications

Confirmation: The Spiritual Wisdom That Has Shaped Our Lives
Edited by Khephra Burns and Susan L. Taylor
Anchor Books

Illuminating Wit, Inspiring Wisdom: Proverbs from Around the World
by Wolfgang Mieder
Prentice Hall Press

The Quotable Spirit: A Treasury of Religious and Spiritual Quotations, from Ancient Times to the 20th century
Compiled and edited by Peter Lorie and Manuela Dunn Mascetti
MacMillan

The Spirit of America: Our Sacred Honor
Edited with commentary by William J. Bennett
Broadman and Holman Publishers

Bartlett's Familiar Quotations
John Bartlett
Little, Brown and Company

MacMillan Dictionary of Quotations
MacMillan Publishers

The Holy Bible
All quotes taken from the King James version

A Book of Saints: True Stories of How They Touch Our Lives
By Anne Gordon
Bantam Books

Confucius: In Life and Legend
By Betty Kelen
Thomas Nelson, Inc.

The Essence of Self-Realization:
The Wisdom of Paramhansa Yogananda
Crystal Clarity, Publishers

The Path:
One Man's Quest on the Only Path There Is
by J. Donald Walters
Crystal Clarity, Publishers

I Came From Joy
Spiritual Songs for Children
Selected by Lorna Knox
Music composed by Donald Walters
Available Spring 2001, CD only

This fun, cheerful recording features many of the songs mentioned in each chapter of the book, *I Came From Joy!* Intended for use as an audio companion to each of the 26 spiritual qualities taught in the book, all of the songs are performed by adults. Designed so that parents and educators can easily teach the songs to children, this music will encourage happiness and self-worth in all children between the pre-school and primary years. This recording can also be used on its own, without the companion book.

Affirmations for Self-Healing
J. Donald Walters
Trade paperback, 126 pages

The affirmations and prayers featured throughout *I Came From Joy!* are adapted from this best-selling book. Intended for adults, *Affirmations for Self-Healing* contains 52 affirmations and prayers that will help you strengthen all of the same qualities—and more— that are taught to children in *I Came From Joy!* For each of the qualities you will find a brief description of its true meaning and importance, an adult-oriented affirmation, and a concluding prayer that reinforces the development of that quality within you. *Affirmations for Self-Healing* is the perfect companion for every adult interested in more seriously developing needed spiritual attitudes and understanding in their own lives.

Education for Life
Preparing Children to Meet the Challenges
J. Donald Walters
Trade paperback, 196 pages.

Here is a constructive alternative to modern education. The author stresses spiritual values and helping children grow toward full maturity learning not only facts, but also innovative principles for better living. Emphasis is placed on the importance of hands-on experiential learning over mere theoretical study. General teaching techniques and curriculum suggestions are offered for each stage of the child's journey. This book is the basis for the Living Wisdom schools and the Education for Life Foundation, a non-profit organization dedicated to training teachers, parents and educators about this breakthrough approach to child development. By encouraging you to see children through their soul qualities, this unique system promises to be a much-needed breath of fresh air.

<u>The Secrets series for Children:</u>

Life's Little Secrets
Little Secrets of Happiness
Little Secrets of Friendship
Little Secrets of Success
J. Donald Walters
Gift books, 72 pages each.

Each *Secrets* book is a collection of profound ideas and important life lessons—one for each day of the month. Each of these four books offers a brief seed-thought that you can read to and discuss with your child each day. Simply and beautifully designed to be of lasting value, each of these inspiring guides is certain to help you and your child develop a greater sense of contentment, friendship, success, and wisdom. Suitable for children ages 6 to 96.

Notes: